THE FOLLIES OF THE WESTERN MIND

For Max's first grandson, whose soul is soon to join this world, and whose name has not yet been chosen.

GRAEME MAXTON

THE FOLLIES OF THE WESTERN MIND

LETTERS FROM MY UNCLE

ARKTOS
LONDON 2025

ΛRKTOS

🌐 Arktos.com 🅕 fb.com/Arktos ◐ 🅞 arktosmedia 🅧 arktosjournal

ISBN

978-1-917646-56-7 (Paperback)
978-1-917646-57-4 (Hardback)
978-1-917646-58-1 (Ebook)

Editing

Constantin von Hoffmeister

Layout and Cover

Tor Westman

CONTENTS

What makes you think?

This book, I hope.

"To thoroughly understand the world, to explain it, to despise it, may be the great thing thinkers do. But I'm only interested in being able to love the world, not to despise it, not to hate it and me, to be able to look upon it and me and all beings with love and admiration and great respect."

— HERMANN HESSE, *Siddhartha*

INTRODUCTION

W HAT IS THINKING? What is it that calls on us to think? Who decides what's good and bad? Do modern societies really understand the meaning of peace? Has science become closed-minded? Does freedom mean the same for everyone? How does language affect the way people think? Is it possible to understand consciousness? What is it like to step back from a world riven by confusion? Is humanity on a collision course with destiny?

This book is about thinking. It is not a philosophy book, a spiritual book, nor a medical book, though it is a little bit of each. It is mostly about how people in the West think, and about how they don't think.

Those who live in the West have developed a closed mindset, bereft of spiritual freedom, and it is leading humanity into a dead end: the risks are existential. Their thinking has become boxed in, inflexible and blinkered. Like a deep-sea diver's suit, Western thinking is weighed down, with restricted movement, and an outlook in only one direction. It has become stifling and constraining. Western minds have become trapped, while another world exists outside.

This book doesn't offer a way out of this prison of the mind. As the final chapter explains, it is up to each of us to find a way. The book offers instead some of the tools needed to escape, some hammers and spanners to pry open the bars.

The way out of this mental gaol is both simple and difficult. It is simple because it only requires some thought. It is difficult because it requires people to understand where they are in this prison. It requires them to look at the world a little differently, to question deeply held beliefs and ideas. It requires them to understand that the way they view the world is not the only way. It requires them to see that there are alternatives, and that some of these might actually be better.

INTRODUCTION

WHAT IS THINKING? What is it that calls on us to think? Who decides what's good and bad? Do modern societies really understand the meaning of peace? Has science become closed-minded? Does freedom mean the same for everyone? How does language affect the way people think? Is it possible to understand consciousness? What is it like to step back from a world riven by confusion? Is humanity on a collision course with destiny?

This book is about thinking. It is not a philosophy book, a spiritual book, nor a medical book, though it is a little bit of each. It is mostly about how people in the West think, and about how they don't think.

Those who live in the West have developed a closed mindset, bereft of spiritual freedom, and it is leading humanity into a dead end: the risks are existential. Their thinking has become boxed in, inflexible and blinkered. Like a deep-sea diver's suit, Western thinking is weighed down, with restricted movement, and an outlook in only one direction. It has become stifling and constraining. Western minds have become trapped, while another world exists outside.

This book doesn't offer a way out of this prison of the mind. As the final chapter explains, it is up to each of us to find a way. The book offers instead some of the tools needed to escape, some hammers and spanners to pry open the bars.

The way out of this mental gaol is both simple and difficult. It is simple because it only requires some thought. It is difficult because it requires people to understand where they are in this prison. It requires them to look at the world a little differently, to question deeply held beliefs and ideas. It requires them to understand that the way they view the world is not the only way. It requires them to see that there are alternatives, and that some of these might actually be better.

CHAPTER 1

A LETTER FROM MY UNCLE, ON FREEDOM

I HAVE AN ELDERLY uncle who still writes letters to me on paper with an envelope. He lives quietly and contemplatively but remains well-informed about the world. He agreed that I could share part of a recent letter he sent me. While I don't agree with everything he says, his views on the present and the past are worth reading. Even if he may sometimes overstate his case, he surely has a point.

∾

Eugendorf, Salzburg
Dezember 1

...I can't help thinking that the present world is separated from the one of my youth by a greater gulf than that which normally separates generations. I can't know for sure, and history suggests I am probably wrong, because every generation tends to think like this. The flow of progress is constant, and one generation inevitably overtakes another. After a time neither can understand the other. And yet I cannot help but feel that everything has changed more rapidly in the last few decades, as if history had accelerated more than in the past.

1

I want to explain this thought in a little more detail, and tell you how I see this unpleasant revolution of the zeitgeist. I want to write it down for myself as much as for you.

In a nutshell, I see four strange paradoxes.

There has been a great decline in people's freedom and this change has made them much less happy. It has made them prisoners in their own minds, and prey to the whims of big companies and the state. I worry that people are being reprogrammed inside their heads without them being aware of it.

I don't want to sing any praises for the old days. I know that in every age there is a small proportion of good and useful achievements. As Hermann Hesse so eloquently puts it, in every age there is one thinker for every thousand talkers, one true believer for every thousand who are soulless, one person who appreciates beauty for every philistine. Perhaps life was not better in the past. But on the whole it seems to me that until a few decades ago people had more light-heartedness and joy in their lives.

People seem to be so pressured today, so driven by the opinions of those they don't know, and may not even like them if they ever met them. How is it that so many lives can be directed by strangers? People shout about their personal freedom and yet their online accounts know their every thought. How is it that their lives are spent feeding the profits of a few big companies and they do not see that? It is the first of my paradoxes. So many people appear to act out of self-love and yet, in reality, almost everything they do is for the gain of others. They have very little freedom of their own, though they fervently believe they do. Their lives are shouted out for others to witness, and yet few of the people they shout at really care. These other people only care about what others think too. Is it surprising that almost no one seems happy?

Those old questions about the roots of our existence seem to have been entirely forgotten or made into entertainment, something for every breeze of fashion. There is no longer any silence, no ability to wait, no distinction between big and small.

All around, people talk endlessly about trivialities, about empty personalities. There is constant noise, and yet any awareness of life, and what it means, doesn't come like this. It can only come when there is time for thought and reflection. Knowledge and learning have been commoditised and stored on machines for instant access. This is paradox two. All this knowledge is freely available and yet it is delivered in a way that seems intended to block understanding. The information is heavily manipulated and controlled, censored by a few big companies in America. In the day-to-day, it is not insight and facts that are fed to people but opinions, dressed as facts, which together form a simplified worldview that is a poor reflection of reality. With the advent of AI it has become even harder to know what is true.

It seems to me that all this is deliberate: the endless flow of small thoughts, the spread of a pre-determined and highly defined reality, and the blurring of truth, is done with a purpose. It is done to take freedom of thought away from people, to stop them considering the world around them, to stop them trying to understand it themselves. This makes people easier to control. It is easier to make them worry, which makes them cautious, to make them vote in certain ways, to make them hate and build them into a froth, and profit from them. It is a huge piece of trickery, like using mirrors to create a fake reality.

Control of the thought narrative even extends to the right of people to control their own destiny. Here we are in the 21st century, and people still have no right to choose the date of their own death, surely the most fundamental of freedoms. The state decides instead, and regulates the process stringently. This is an issue I think about frequently, as you know. I suspect future generations will be horrified that such cruel and inhuman thinking was ever possible, that all those who long for peace were made to suffer so much.

It also appears as if everything that is done by people must bear fruit almost immediately. Everything has become a competition, even the baking of a scone. The speed of perceived achievement has become much more important than the fruits of success, just as the sense of winning has eradicated the pleasure of working together, of cooperation. It is like trying to accelerate the growth of a plant before understanding what makes it grow, or why.

Everywhere, people are burrowing around the roots, experimenting and exploiting what they see in the hope of instant reward, and that makes me suspicious. Nothing is left for those who want to think. Nothing is left to remain silent about. Everything is discussed, laid bare, illuminated with that distinct and approved light, with every academic study published hungry to be accepted as knowledge. The brightest people, those toiling PhD students, are stuck in libraries burrowing into the most pointless minutiae while the world's most serious problems are largely ignored. It is either that or the brightest have been drugged into financial compliance by soulless rewards. Again, this all seems as if by design to me. It removes choice, eradicates considered views that do not fall into the specified prescription, simplifies what should not be simplified, removes that skill of considering the long term, and the purpose of life. It eradicates the pleasure that comes from seeing the beauty of the world. It all takes us further away from ourselves.

I am sure it was not like that before. I am sure I am not misremembering.

More than a decade ago there was a campaign in Spain for the right to be forgotten, and that young Austrian, Max Schrems, launched a case against Facebook. Not long after, Edward Snowden was forced into exile in Russia. Do you remember? These people wanted to protect long-won fundamental rights, *real* pillars of freedom. Without the right to forget or live anonymously people cannot be free. They can be manipulated, unable to move on, always haunted by their past. If they are watched and tracked, they feel constrained if they ever want to say what they really think, worried about where their views will be logged, on what website their names will appear. They are unable to live their lives as previous generations, because they are not given the freedom to think what they wish.

What has happened since these cases were in the news? It has got worse. Almost everything is monitored and watched, even doorbells, refrigerators and wrist watches now listen. Cameras and microphones are installed everywhere, on phones and computers, and switched on by programmes you don't even know are there. Phones know everywhere you go and, if you forget your phone, your car tracks you instead, or those cameras installed on every lamppost. Every computer keystroke is logged. And all of this data is stored in Nevada and other places. Every search on Google is saved for eternity, every post and 'like' on Facebook is used to profile you.

Yet people just shrug, and say that they have nothing to hide. Try telling that to those whose details were recorded in the Netherlands before the Second World War and they ended up in concentration camps.

With so much surveillance it's like living with a family member or a stranger always standing at your shoulder. Imagine your mother or a neighbour, always watching what you do, listening to what you say, guessing what you are thinking, knowing your future plans and recording the details of your most intimate passions and experiences.

How can this be called freedom?

With cash now disappearing, everything people buy is tracked too, from a bottle of gin to some condoms. I heard recently that a UK bank had sent messages to its customers telling them off for their bad diets because the apps knew what they bought at the supermarket. A bank telling you how to live your life! And all this is tracked and recorded and stored forever too.

Who is doing all this tracking? You know, of course. We've talked about this often. It's the state, and not just your own nation's state but the US government as well: it collects all it needs through a handful of privately-owned but government-influenced technology businesses. Were these half dozen companies Chinese or Russian, there would be an outcry. They have risen to have such dominant control in just a few decades, risen like a winged Mercury, and now they have such unconstrained power over everyone's lives. Because they are American, it seems, almost no one sees there is a problem. The country responsible for more civilian deaths, more wars, more regime changes and more snooping than any other in the last 50 years, the country that refuses to comply with important international conventions, which wants to give an amnesty to soldiers accused of war crimes, and which hounds those who expose its tracking, is viewed as trustworthy by almost everyone for some strange reason. No one says anything. Are they all blind? This is my third paradox: everyone says mass surveillance and a police state are bad, and point to China as a heinous example, and yet they are living in precisely the conditions they claim to oppose.

All this leads to a great gulf between what goes on in the inside of our minds, and what happens on the outside. It divides people from the real world. A consequence is a loss of imagination for many people, which deepens the loss of contentment and humour, and destroys the art of living. Who even talks about *that* today?

Freedom of the mind, which is what freedom originally meant, can only flourish on the foundations of an inner understanding of our relationship to the world around us. The lives of so many people are made worse not just by the constant noise but by the pressure for change. People are not allowed to integrate, to feel at one with the world. Everything is always being thrown away and renewed. This hankering for change makes people poorer; it damages their souls by encouraging a dislike of stability, whether that be one's view of the world, or the love of small everyday objects around us, and nature. No one has time for beauty, and so they remain distant from what matters, from what brings deeper contentment.

In the same way, so many people seem unable to hold onto any belief or inner conviction except at the most superficial level. Everything is black and white.

You and I have talked of this many times, and I apologise for repeating myself. But one glance at any newspaper is enough to see that an agenda is being laid out, like poisoned bird seed for everyone to peck. It is not nourishment that's offered, just intellectual fat, salt and sugar, with mind-warping additives, but it is hungrily consumed nonetheless. The narrative is simple. Growth is good, Russia is bad, China is bad, North Korea is bad, Hungary is not democratic, you should worry about the future and about the climate (but not enough to encourage any useful response to the problem). Don't question the medicines they prescribe, or the political system. Choose the centrist parties, the ones who support business. Don't question democracy, or suggest it might not work. Fret about a world war, and remember that conflict is necessary. Never forget that you are on the right side. There's a new iPhone coming out. Put up Christmas decorations in October. There's a funny new video on TikTok.

It's almost impossible for people to cope with the material challenges we all face, when every second is filled with ideas that sting like nettles. Paradox four: within the cacophony there is a lure that everything should be easy, and that no effort is ever required. The hook is fed that it is easy to know without any need to learn. This creates unhappiness too because it is simply not true. It creates a false ambition in people, a belief that they can know and understand without effort, which can only frustrate them.

Of course, none of this will bring about the end of the world, though it surely stupefies people, dulling their awareness of the risks. It anaesthetises them.

It is this loss of proper understanding, this distance from knowledge, that will be the hardest to repair. Knowledge and effort valued in the past are seen as trivial and silly. They have been replaced by ludicrous aspirations, leading to an ever-thirsty and gnawing discontent with life, a living out of balance.

Not many years ago, families were more anchored to little things and little pleasures, rooted in their own stability. The outside world exerted a powerful draw but it was balanced by a sense of belonging, and that wonderful feeling of home. This created space for thought and the happiness of being together with those who share bonds, with goodwill for communication and conversation.

Of course every family still has its own tone, its secrets, its own language and form of teasing, and that will always be the case. But beyond, outside, the world now lacks colour and cheerfulness. This lack of contentment cannot be replaced by the latest iPhone, a new car or a 30-second video, and yet people have come to think it can…

~

As I said, I don't share all his views. But his comments are surely worthy of some reflection.

This essay was inspired by Hermann Hesse's short story "The Old Days", written in 1907.

CHAPTER 2

WHAT IS THIS THING CALLED THINKING?

Part 1

Paracelsusgasse, München
Jänner 6

Dear nephew,

I hope your trip to Vienna went well.

I've spent most of the last month looking after my books, inspired by my recent trip to Japan. I went to one of the libraries in Tokyo and found the staff taking all the books off the shelves, meticulously turning every page and then putting them back. They said this was to preserve them. Damp is a problem in Japan.

After such a wet autumn, it inspired me to do the same when I got home. Of course, the process took far longer than it should because I was frequently distracted by the books, and by Pushkin. As soon as a shelf was free, he climbed onto it using the ladder, crouched down, and stared at me.

Sometimes, he had a long wait, especially after I came across one particular book which interrupted my work for many days. It's a book[1] I had almost forgotten I had. It's subject? Thinking.

As you might expect, the book got me thinking. I began to wonder why there is so little academic work on what is called thinking.

I've been making notes and I thought you might be interested. They're in four sections, though there is overlap. The first section is about the physical process of thinking. The next is on what I've called the ethereal process of what is called thinking, the hardest to define. The third part is on the currency of thinking, how it is boxed in and directed. The last part is on the role language plays. I've added references where I can. Some of what I am sending is still in note form. I'll write it up and turn it into a lecture once I've finished sorting my books.

There are lots more questions than answers.

1. Notes on the physical process of what is called thinking

There appears to be a great deal of research on neural pathways and the biological functions of the brain. Yet very little is really understood. There is almost no research on the process of thinking. That seems remiss, careless even. Everyone thinks almost constantly. Thinking determines everything people say and do. Yet very little serious work has been put into analysing what thinking is and how it works.

What exactly is this thing called thinking?

Scientists say thinking occurs in the brain, and that our bodies are mostly controlled by what our minds decide. Yet the body also appears to have some level of distributed intelligence. Not everything depends on the brain. Many bodily functions appear to work themselves, without the brain's intervention. As long as people eat, rest, and exercise, their bodies' cells do their job, and renew themselves, without

---

1   Heidegger, Martin (1968). *What Is Called Thinking?* (*Was heißt Denken*) Translated by Gray, J. Glenn. New York: HarperPerennial.

instructions from the brain. The cardiac systems of people who are brain dead can continue to function for several weeks.[2]

This raises a tantalising question. Is the brain the source of *everything* we call thinking?

Scientists can measure wave patterns in the brain. When they cut bits of the brain away, they find this leads to physical, behavioural and memory changes, but not always. It seems to vary. Doctors can send signals electrically and chemically to the brain and get a response. The brain can move prosthetic limbs. Scientists say they can track how the brain processes information.

But none of this proves the brain is thinking. Computers process information, but they don't think.

Do scientists consider the brain, the mind, and consciousness one entity because they can't prove empirically there's a difference? Or don't they ask that question? Where does the soul fit? Or is the soul an idea that belongs to the Church, so no one can question it, and science can ignore it?

Aristotle believed all living creatures have a soul, even plants. It is their essence, he thought. Animals have what he calls a "sensitive soul", humans a "rational soul" and plants a "vegetative soul". While humans have all three souls, rationality is what distinguishes them from other species, he said. While the body is mortal and made from the stars, the intellectual soul, the human soul, is eternal. It is God's breath, said Paracelsus, who believed there were four souls, not three, adding the "spiritual soul".

The vegetative soul governs nutrition, growth and reproduction.

[Vegetal Soul.] Vegetal, the first of the three distinct faculties, is defined to be 'a substantial act of an organical body, by which it is nourished, augmented, and begets another like unto itself.' Three operations are specified. The first is nutrition, whose object is nourishment, meat, drink, and the

2   Al-Shammri S, Nelson RF, Madavan R, Subramaniam TA, Swaminathan TR. "Survival of cardiac function after brain death in patients in Kuwait". Eur Neurol. 2003;49(2):90–3. doi: 10.1159/000068506. PMID: 12584416.

like; his organ the liver in sensible creatures; in plants, the root or sap. His office is to turn the nutriment into the substance of the body nourished, which he performs by natural heat. This nutritive operation hath four other subordinate functions or powers belonging to it — attraction, retention, digestion, expulsion.

Augmentation is the second operation or power of the vegetal faculty: to the increasing of it in quantity, according to all dimensions, long, broad, thick, and to make it grow till it come to his due proportion and perfect shape.

The last of these vegetal faculties is generation, which begets another by means of seed, like unto itself, to the perpetual preservation of the species.

— ROBERT BURTON, *The Anatomy of Melancholy* (1621),
The First Section, Subject V, edited for clarity

As an aside for a moment, Burton's book contains many interesting sections, including an analysis of how the Devil, witches and old age cause depression. It says that eating cabbage causes bad dreams by sending black vapours to the brain. What people once believed appears amusing to us now. But what will future generations think of the current era's ideas, I wonder? Which beliefs will be regarded as laughable? Surely not none.

The sensitive soul, which all animals have, gives them common sense, an appetite, judgement, memory, breath, imagination, and motion as well as the five "outward" senses of sight, taste, scent, touch and sound. Some refer also to a sixth sense, "titillation". Speech is also regarded as a sixth "external" sense, according to Lullius. The ability to imagine, originally called *phantasie*, was thought to be especially unusual because it is also active during sleep; indeed, this is where it is most free. It was also thought to be most pronounced in those suffering from melancholy or depression.

The rational soul was thought to be the home of understanding and free will. This is where sense, experience, intelligence, faith, suspicion, opinion and science were thought to reside, along with art, prudency (the ability to govern oneself and have good judgement), and wisdom. Plato believed all these abilities were innate.

Do you remember Suzanna Grüber, my friend who lives in Graz? She says she has suffered pain all her life, spiritual pain. You know how sensitive she is, how much she sees the world in ways the rest of us don't, how much she hears, and how much she hates crowds and needs tranquillity. She thinks her pain is because her soul was misaligned at birth. It's an interesting idea. She says there are people who suffer from the opposite problem; they don't communicate with their souls at all, or recognise them. They ignore them and suffer pain as a result.

Is there dualism? Are the mind and body separate? Countless philosophers and many religious thinkers believe so, though the prevailing Western consensus appears so often to deny or ignore the idea. The thought that when people die everything dies with them, including their thoughts, is commonly held. That may be because those who believe that don't think of course, as Suzanna says.

Could consciousness be eternal? Might it live for ever as Aristotle, Buddhists, many religions and some philosophers say? Is there a link between human thought and string theory or M-theory in particle physics? Could human thinking be linked to one of the other dimensions that have been identified?

Could the theory of quantum entanglement offer any insight into what we call thinking? Physicists know it takes millions of years for light to travel vast distances and yet the theory of quantum entanglement says two electrons can communicate instantly, no matter where they are in the universe, because they are always linked. Is it possible that this communication could impact the trillions of connections and 100 billion neurons that make up the human brain? Could it have any impact on how people think, or could think?

Does thinking have mass or energy? Scientists generally believe thinking is the result of electrical impulses, which have mass and energy. But could this be because scientists don't recognise anything without these properties?

According to the "global workspace"[3] theory of consciousness, incoming sensory information is first processed in parts of the brain without us being aware of it. People only become aware of what's happening when the signals are sent to a network of neurons, which are then distributed across the brain. This raises a difficult question: are the electrical impulses doctors track on their oscilloscopes caused by thinking, or are they the result of thinking being communicated from somewhere else to the brain? Could the wave patterns be a physical response to thoughts, not the result of thinking itself? If so, this raises an even more difficult question: could thoughts also come from outside us? Is it possible that the processing part of the brain receives messages not just from the body's sensors and the environment, but also from somewhere else? Could there be a field of consciousness around us, a property of the universe, like mass, or energy, that our brains are tuned into?

As I'll explain, this is not as fanciful an idea as it might seem.

If this were true, could this mean the God-created-the-universe theory is basically correct, just misunderstood? There is no supreme being. There is no single creator. But there is a living, conscious universe, developing and evolving. Could there be a universal consciousness present in all living things? Is this what gives us life? Does each of us have the whole universe within us, just as a fragment of a hologram contains the entire picture within it?

This theme was also picked up by Paracelsus. He believed that everything that exists in the universe is replicated with each of us. We all possess our own "Jupiter, oak tree, gold, and essence of every other being in the universe". He argued that the "dust of the earth" written about in the Bible in Genesis 2:7, which Paracelsus called the "limbus", and which was used to create humans, contains every essence of the material universe within it. Humans contain the seeds of everything that exists.

---

3   https://doi.org/10.1016/S0079-6123(05)50004-9.

~

It's clear, I think, that some of our ideas emerge from past thinking. The mind takes another step along a path that has been created in our memories. Other thoughts are harder to explain. They seem to appear spontaneously, unlinked to anything else. A sudden impulse to go somewhere or see someone. A sudden desire to take a different path in life. How to explain where these thoughts come from? Where do these random ideas, those that can't be tied to any obvious stimulus, emerge? How to explain impulses that appear out of the blue? Where do entirely new ideas spring from? Could our minds really be linked to some invisible strand of existence not yet discovered?

Or is everything exactly as science suggests? Is the world, as Schopenhauer said, our own idea?Does everything we perceive depend entirely on our consciousness for its existence? *"However immeasurable and massive the world may be, its existence hangs by one single thread: the individual consciousness in which it exists."*[4]

Is reality not as we believe but "a controlled hallucination", as some neuroscientists say?

If some ideas are communicated by a universal consciousness, if they are detected by the brain in some way, might this explain the theory of multiple discovery, when different people make similar discoveries even when they are far apart? The discovery of magnetism, oxygen, and calculus for example, each of which was identified by people in unconnected, geographically disparate societies around the same time. Perhaps discovery is not the right word here. It is too often confused with invention and breakthrough. Magnetism, oxygen, and calculus have always existed. Perhaps it is better to say they were "revealed" in different places simultaneously.

---

4   Arthur Schopenhauer, 1818, *The World as Will and Idea*, chapter 1, volume 2.

Studies show people's brains can be synchronised. The brains of lovers kissing, chess players, computer gamers, and musicians[5] will gradually adapt until they have the same wave patterns, as if each is tuning into some universal frequency. Our ability to do this can even be improved. Studies show people can learn[6] to coordinate their brains with others, to make them work in harmony. How is this possible if everything is held within our heads?

Do all people think in the same way? Is the process the same for everyone? Logic suggests not. People think in different ways and not simply because they have different values, opinions, and levels of intelligence. Thinking appears to be an aspect of individual character. Different people draw different conclusions from the same information. Is this because their minds are "wired" differently? Is the activity of the brain, the process of what we call thinking, similar to the way people move? Individuals run, walk, and move in ways that are unique, which is why modern surveillance systems watch people's gait. If people move their bodies in unique ways, do they also think in unique ways?

What makes one mind superior to another? Is a superior mind determined by the number of neurons, the inter-linkages connecting the lobes of the brain, or the speed of information transfer? Can people improve their ability to think; can they make their minds better or stronger? Can someone become more intelligent? People can improve memory and recall. The brain's function also decays with age. Can people boost their intellect or fundamentally improve the process of their thinking? Or is intelligence hard-wired from birth?

5   Lindenberger, U., Li, SC., Gruber, W. et al. "Brains swinging in concert: cortical phase synchronization while playing guitar". BMC Neurosci 10, 22 (2009). https://doi.org/10.1186/1471-2202-10-22.

6   Max Plank Institute interview February 6, 2024, Inter-Brain Synchronization: "My fascination with the topic continues to this day!" Interview with Viktor Müller on the occasion of his retirement: https://www.mpib-berlin.mpg. de/1805490/pm-2024-feburary-lip. Accessed January 27, 2025.

I ask again: what is it, this thing called thinking? What is it that allows a material brain to generate something we call consciousness, to generate that palpable, invisible thing we call awareness? Is it possible to measure this thing called thinking? Is there such a thing as big thinking or small thinking, just as there are big hands and small hands?

Stanley Rose, a neighbour, ended up in hospital with cirrhosis. He was very ill and treated with strong painkillers and other chemicals. When he got home he spent three days sitting up in bed talking nonsense. Never slept, constantly recited random parts of stories from his life, endlessly. He told me about it afterwards. He said the most frightening thing was that he knew he was doing it. He couldn't control it. He knew he appeared mad. He was trapped inside his mind.

How do those labelled mad think? How does it differ from everyone else? Is there a sliding scale of thinking, from sanity to madness? Could it be measured? How do some people have special thinking skills? How do some people see numbers and music as colours? How is it possible for some of those with autism, some people born with a genetic variation, some people who suffer a brain injury and some of those afflicted by a disease of the central nervous system, to have enhanced skills? Do they actually have greater skills, or does their affliction just make a universal ability visible? Could everyone have these enhanced faculties hidden within?

Why do some forms of autism develop in later life, or appear suddenly? How can some parts of the brain appear to heal or restructure? What does this mean for what is called thinking?

Why do only a small percentage of savants appear to have enhanced abilities? Why are there far more male than female savants, a ratio of 6:1? Why are there six times more male savants with their special thinking skills than women? Does this suggest the female thinking process is different from the male? Or is it, as a super-intelligent autistic friend in Munich suggests, because of a failure to diagnose autism in women properly?

The most common type of savants are called calendrical. They have the ability to calculate and memorise dates and days of the week with great accuracy almost instantly. How do they access this information or know how to do this? Other savants have exceptional abilities in memory, art, music, mathematics or arithmetic. Some have an enhanced ability to see or manipulate 2- or 3-dimensional objects. Others instinctively know the correct time, down to the precise minute. These skills arguably have roots in numbers, in mathematics, symmetry and natural harmonies. Is this significant? Why do savants often suffer from intellectual, physical or social impairments? Why are they motorically handicapped?

What role does simultaneous thinking play? People think in multiple ways at the same time. They drive a car, maintain a conversation, and listen to the radio while thinking about a relationship, what to eat for lunch, or the weather. Does everyone do this to the same degree? Can some people think in multiple dimensions and others with only a few strands of thought?

Does not-thinking offer any clues about this thing we call thinking? Thoughts appear to constantly pour into our minds from all sides. They are almost impossible to stop. Not-thinking, clearing the mind of every thought, is extremely difficult. Try meditating. Stopping the stream of noise takes a lot of work, though it can be improved with practice. By focussing completely on a task, thinking can be funnelled to dampen or silence other frequencies. But thoughts still try to interrupt. Some of these relate to time, or what comes next. Others appear to be random and unconnected. Why?

What of dreams? Are dreams thinking too? What happens during that delicious time in the morning, between wakefulness and sleep, when the mind keeps drifting between two states, where there is rational thought interspersed with random ideas and images, where the mind wants to wake and sleep equally? How does thinking in a mind that is awake differ from thinking in a mind that is asleep? How does this differ from a mind when it dreams? And does thinking in sleep differ from thinking in a coma, or other forms of unconsciousness? What happens to thinking when someone is under anaesthetic? Is there thinking at every level of consciousness or only some levels? What determines the difference?

Why do some people wake up after many years in a coma? Why do they sometimes go back into a coma after appearing to recover? How do some people emerge from what is medically classified as a 'vegetative state'?[7] Why do some people in a persistent vegetative state appear to be awake and yet have no awareness of their surroundings? Unlike those in a coma, people in a vegetative state can sometimes chew and swallow, sleep (interestingly, with their eyes open), move, respond to stimuli and make sounds. Yet they are not considered to be conscious.

This smacks into an enormous and eternal question: what is consciousness?

I find it amazing that after so many years of study, and so many centuries of scientific progress, no one knows what it is.

I remember meeting someone at a dinner party in Singapore many years ago who had just qualified as an anaesthetist. I asked her about how the process worked, about what exactly induces unconsciousness. She told me that doctors don't know exactly. They understand what they need to do to create the effect necessary for treatment, and they get it wrong sometimes. But they don't fully understand how anaesthesia works, what it does to the mind, or why such a wide range of seemingly unrelated chemicals can create similar effects.

Isn't that astonishing?

The cerebellum contains about three-quarters of the brain's neurons and yet it seems to have almost nothing to do with consciousness. While it's been shown that damage to parts of the thalamus or the brain stem can result in permanent unconsciousness, scientists don't know why. Are these parts the power socket to the brain, they

---

7   Quinones-Ossa, G. A., Durango-Espinosa, Y. A., Janjua, T. et al. "Persistent vegetative state: an overview". Egypt J Neurosurg 36, 9 (2021). https://doi.org/10.1186/s41984-021-00111-3.

ask, or something more? In the last few decades, new research suggests consciousness depends on the ways different parts of the brain communicate with each other, especially the cortex. But this is just an observation.

Most research work on the brain has been about perception, cognition, learning and behaviour, concepts that are relatively simple to understand and study. Papers on the more complex question of defining the life force are less common. I found several that come back to my earlier comments on a universal consciousness though, with some even asking if an electron could have consciousness.

What happens to thinking during sex? Studies at Rutgers University show there is a change in consciousness during orgasm, with parts of the brain shutting down, creating a sense of loss of control. Having an orgasm with a partner creates a slightly altered brain state from having one alone. Research[8] in this area is now looking at how the brain patterns could be replicated, not for pleasure, but to help people ease pain.

What of other species? Do they think the same way? There is a commonly held belief in most of the world that humans are a more intelligent species, the most intelligent. Aristotle thought so. Many people even think other species and animals are not self-aware. To me, this is complete nonsense.

---

8   Komisaruk BR, Whipple B, Crawford A, Liu WC, Kalnin A, Mosier K. "Brain activation during vaginocervical self-stimulation and orgasm in women with complete spinal cord injury: fMRI evidence of mediation by the vagus nerves". Brain Res. 2004 Oct 22;1024(1–2):77–88. doi: 10.1016/j.brainres.2004.07.029. PMID: 15451368.

Studies show that animals can communicate over vast distances in real time. Whales communicate[9] using particle motion.[10] A US study[11] has shown that rats can share information over great distances too. A rat in America was able to help a rat in Brazil solve a puzzle. Scientists wired their brains up and then plugged them into the internet. One rat helped the other through a maze for a reward. This begs a question too: did this communication need the internet? The internet is a man-made communication system. Could it work without the internet?

Wohlleben[12] says trees communicate with each other and with their environment. Do they think? Plants communicate using volatile organic compounds (VOCs).[13] Inter-plant communication protects them from environmental threats. Humans communicate using sound waves. Voices generate sound waves that are picked up by the ears. Do dogs, deer and other mammals use olfactory communication systems? Is their language based on scent? Could some species use brain waves to talk? Cats can anticipate where their owners are going to be. How do they do this?

Have I ever told you about a cat I had as a boy? His name was Tigger. I have a picture of him on my desk. He was a remarkable cat.

I used to come home from school on the bus. Because of after-school activities, I would come back at all sorts of different times. I'd also take different buses, which went to different locations near to

---

9   Mooney TA, Kaplan MB, Lammers MO. "Singing whales generate high levels of particle motion: implications for acoustic communication and hearing?" Biol Lett. 2016 Nov;12(11):20160381. doi: 10.1098/rsbl.2016.0381. PMID: 27807249; PMCID: PMC5134030.

10 https://doi.org/10.1111/2041-210X.12544.

11 Pais-Vieira, M., Lebedev, M., Kunicki, C. et al. "A Brain-to-Brain Interface for Real-Time Sharing of Sensorimotor Information". Sci Rep 3, 1319 (2013). https://doi.org/10.1038/srep01319.

12 Wohlleben, P. (2016). The Hidden Life of Trees. [United States], Greystone Books.

13 Aratani, Y., Uemura, T., Hagihara, T. et al. "Green leaf volatile sensory calcium transduction in Arabidopsis". Nat Commun 14, 6236 (2023). https://doi.org/10.1038/s41467-023-41589-9.

where we lived. This meant I could approach the house from several different directions, at different times of day. Yet on many occasions Tigger would be waiting for me at the correct bus stop at the correct time. He'd walk home with me, often crossing several busy roads by himself. He seemed to know where I was going to be in advance, and know when I was going to get there. The funniest thing was that on the walk back he'd never walk beside me, as a dog would. He'd always walk on the opposite pavement, on the other side of the road, as if he wasn't really there for me. But he was. He'd stop every so often and watch me.

When we lived in Zurich we had another cat, a black and white one, and it did exactly the same thing. Didn't you meet her when you came to see us? We called her Schatzi. Just like Tigger, she'd regularly come and meet us from the cable car we took home, the *Seilbahn*. She'd be sitting there, at the top of the steps, at all sorts of times of day, at exactly the time we got there. Then she'd walk home with us, not on the other side of the road, but 20 metres in front. Cats always hate to give the impression of being dependent on those they deign to let feed them. Whenever we were away for more than a few days, or whenever your aunt came back after her month-long trips to Hong Kong, she'd *always* be there, waiting.

Quite remarkable.

Notes for further research

- Look at the impact of light waves on the brain. A research paper shows the brain can detect infrared light not visible to the eyes.[14]

- Theories on thinking seem thin. Scientists and philosophers understand little about the process of thinking. Almost nothing to explain how the process works, or why some thoughts are retained

---

14 Thomson, E., Carra, R. & Nicolelis, M. "Perceiving invisible light through a somatosensory cortical prosthesis". Nat Commun 4, 1482 (2013). https://doi.org/10.1038/ncomms2497.

and others are not. Most descriptions of thinking liken the brain to a computer or machine. This doesn't seem a good analogy. The human neural network is much more complex. Thoughts don't emerge in one area. They are spread throughout the network.

• Might it be shown that telepathy is possible according to the laws of quantum physics?

• What can MDMA, psychedelics and other drugs tell us? Psilocybin causes acute changes in how people perceive time, space, and the self. Functional connectivity within brain networks becomes less synchronized. The effect can last three weeks. A Cornell paper[15] says psychedelics reduce the energy needed to switch between different activity states. What does this mean for thinking? Emotions can be enhanced, such as bliss or fear. It's possible to induce vast changes in perceptions of reality. Patients report a sense of 'visiting' alternate realities or dimensions. Others report similarities to near-death experiences and increased empathy. This raises another very difficult question: what is reality?

• Peking Uni paper. Top desk drawer, blue folder.

• Rostov analysis — green notebook, marked page.

≈

Heavens! What a pile of notes I've accumulated on the physical process of thinking! It is far larger than I thought. If I send you my other notes now, on the process of thinking, the currency of thinking, and the linguistic aspects. there will be far too much paper for the envelope. I would also like to do some more work on these other topics before I let you read them.

---

15 Singleton, S. P., Luppi, A. I., Carhart-Harris, R. L. et al. "Receptor-informed network control theory links LSD and psilocybin to a flattening of the brain's control energy landscape". Nat Commun 13, 5812 (2022). https://doi.org/10.1038/s41467-022-33578-1.

So I'll send you what I have for now, and write again soon when I've collected my other thoughts.

With much love
Max

PS. At the bottom of my notes are some pages written by Natasha. I found them between two books of photographs. They must have been written when she stayed with us in Shanghai, when she was 16, not long before the accident. I thought you should have them.

∾

CHAPTER 3

ON WAR, AND THE MEANING OF PEACE

M Y UNCLE HAS agreed that I can share part of a recent letter he
sent me. The theme is war, and the meaning of peace.

~

Cultoquhey, Gilmerton
February 5

My dear nephew,

I write a few days after returning from Asia where I spent several weeks with old friends over Christmas enjoying Japanese and
Szechuan food again. My trip gave me the chance to see how Hong
Kong has changed since Beijing enforced its will (and the answer is
not much, at least superficially), and to reflect a little on the unchanging rhetoric about the risks of war between Taiwan and China. As in
Europe, there is endless talk in Asia about the chance of conflict. While
the Europeans are told to fear an escalation with Russia, the people in
Japan, Taiwan and many other countries in Asia are expected to fret
about the existential risks posed by China and North Korea.

It is all so much nonsense. Whatever differences exist between
these nations, there is no reason for people to die. There are solutions

that can be found, and will eventually need to be found. Talk of war appears to be designed mostly to keep people afraid, to make them supine, and easy to manipulate.

During the last few years especially, it seems to me that the pro-war rhetoric has become louder, and that any opposition based on principle has become harder to voice. There has been a hardening of hearts, a forgetting of the past, with less reasoned comment and more unsound thinking. If history teaches us anything, these signs suggest there is trouble ahead. The media in Europe is filled with posts and articles mocking and blaming Russia, while the feeds in Asia are sprinkled with opinion pieces designed to encourage a fear of China. That small minority who love war, who profit from it, who view it as inevitable and cleansing, are gaining the upper hand again.

As you know, I am deeply opposed to all this. War is the animal force that holds humanity back, which constrains civilisation. But such thinking appears less these days, and is often actively dismissed. Already, there are neighbours who turn away from me. Conformists never fail to heap scorn on those who choose to walk alone when the earth begins to shake, when orgies of hatred and morbid nationalism spread, like the roots of a well-nourished weed.

I flew back through Germany where I found an interesting article[1] written by a Russian exile, a man whose conscience had forced him out of his home country. He wrote about the rising tide of anti-Russian sentiment across Europe. It has taken on ridiculous proportions, he said. He had even come under attack for having a longing for Russian soup. Russian soups are the products of Russian imperialism, he was told, and quite seriously, because they are made from recipes stolen from colonised lands. He said that just speaking Russian is enough for someone to be reported to the authorities as suspicious, and that people are even refusing to attend concerts if they feature Russian composers.

---

1 "Wenn sogar Suppe zur Waffe wird", *Die Welt*, 27 Dec. 2024.

How can avoiding something that touches the soul, which crosses human divides like that, be in any way useful? All such stupidity does is make the inevitable reconciliation between Europe and Russia more difficult. It drives a wedge into good thinking.

There is nothing new in all this of course. It is exactly what happened in the First World War, when the petty divisions stoked beforehand made peace so much harder to achieve.

It's easy to think I'm being political, or taking sides, but that's not so. On the stage of the world's theatre it's always the political problems that everyone focuses on, when the issues of greatest concern are really the innermost ideas that force humanity to sit before the judgement of its own conscience.

If we are to move forward as a species, it's at times like these when people need to listen to the voices of rationality within them, even when this brings hostility and laughter. The demands of the world and the pull of our souls are always hard to reconcile: that is our test. Yet so many people seem unable to learn even the most basic lessons. They rally to whichever flag they see, lacking any sense of measured judgement. They seem to have nothing more than a superficial understanding of history and give little thought to human purpose.

At school, I remember being asked to write an essay on war. "What features of human nature are most aroused by war?" was the question. Of course, my answer was hopeless. I knew nothing about the consequences of war at that time, nor anything about the cycles that drive these festivals of death.

I've thought about that question a good deal since, and I can see that what matters most is not the behaviour of those who actually fight wars with guns and missiles, or even the politicians who direct them. What matters more is the behaviour of the bungalow intellectuals, the doctors, teachers, artists, technologists and writers, those who might be expected to think a little more deeply.

These people seem to be so easily swayed by superficial ideas. It's these thin-lipped intellectuals, who avoid Russian soup and hungrily digest frothy articles designed to fuel their petty indignation, that are the main problem. They always fail to ask about the views of those on the other side, and swallow every conformist message they are fed unquestioningly. They unthinkingly embrace the idea that their latest foes have suddenly transformed themselves into aggressive brain-washed madmen overnight. The literature and art of the newest target of these people's venom is swiftly washed from their minds. These supposedly educated and considered people rarely take even a moment to reflect on the transition in their thinking. They fail to see what has happened within their own minds, or remind themselves what they once believed.

I find it quite remarkable, this destructive confusion of these single-story intellectuals, this easy transition in their thinking. It suggests that their ideas never had any solidity, that their views and opinions, while fervently expressed, were always like warm wax.

A shocking number of these floppy-brained societal pillars even start spewing their own hot bile, with bloodthirsty social media posts that spread outrageous half-truths and foment hatred. Can it really be the function of otherwise intelligent people to make a situation worse than it already is? Is war not ugly and deplorable enough without these blancmange-brained people pissing their tepid self-brew into the stew?

All this reflects a failure to think, a mental laziness that may be perfectly pardonable in a soldier, or in those drones who fire drones into Russia at the press of a button, but it ill-becomes those who regard themselves thoughtful, who once said they believed in humanitarian action, when it was convenient for them. Now that these ideals involve some deeper thought, now that they are a matter of life and death to those firing the guns, these people abandon what they claimed were their principles and sing instead the hymn their neighbours and the warmongers want to hear. I find it both comic and tragic that those who once said they strongly opposed the death penalty, should quickly relegate what was best in them to dust. What happened to their inner freedom, their intellectual conscience, to their sense of humanity? Was it never really there?

When I say these things, friends sometimes accuse me of ivory-tower intellectualism and tell me I should hold my tongue. Yet this is surely the time to speak up. Is that not what the imperatives of justice and decency demand? At some point, a conflict always comes to an end and, unless the other side has been completely annihilated, there needs to be cultural exchange again. Is it not necessary to remember that, to preserve some foundation for peace, to continuously look for ways to build bridges instead of demolishing every possible path to a better future?

The elimination of war is surely humanity's ultimate goal. The foundations of any lasting human civilisation have to be built on humanity suppressing its animalistic instincts, and following considered impulses instead. The pillars need to be built on a sense of historic shame, with imagination and understanding. The simple idea that life is worth living, and worth preserving, is what history is trying to tell us.

Of course, the politicians and the media have a lot to answer for too. Government ministers in Germany, the US, and Britain blithely talk about their desire to end the conflict while simultaneously agreeing to deliver more weapons. They tell us that the time for negotiations is not yet at hand, and blame Russia. There is no thought for balance, no love, no sense of humanity, no real thought for those people who are expected to sacrifice their precious lives.

Nothing in what these politicians say serves any sort of ideal. It is not the product of any faith, or any awareness of human need. Everything is a transaction: every perceived bad deed by the other side has to be punished by some balancing action. Why? Why is this necessary? Is it really useful to litter Ukraine and Russia with the dead and dying, to shatter so many people's lives, and char and desecrate their soils? While a few people and a few big companies profit from weapons sales, and a few politicians sit proudly for a moment on the shoulders of the shallow-minded, the voices of the wounded, the accusations of the mothers, lovers and children, and the cries of the desperate, go unheard.

If the armchair thinkers could hear these other voices, might that not open their minds and allow them to weigh the value of the wars they fuel? Were they forced to experience the misery of a single day of war themselves, on the front line, might they not stop and think for a moment?

Perhaps that is where they should be sent, so they can learn. If those soft-headed people could hear the voice of reality, even briefly, they might consider their duty to humankind, and understand that all those billions being spent, those empty victories, those battles over trifling pieces of territory, and a thousand other things that prolong the conflict are causing untold torment to so many people. Then they might find the courage to condemn this useless war, because what has been achieved is not worth the price. If they did this, then these weak-minded people might finally stand above their contemporaries in the eyes of humankind.

History shows that people have always lived at the expense of others, that every group fears and hates every other. So far, life has been mostly defined by wars, which is easy. It is peace that is difficult. Peace is not some paradise. It is not simple coexistence by mutual agreement. It is not the absence of war. It is something humanity does not yet know, something it has yet to discover. Peace is a state that is infinitely complex, unstable and fragile. Humanity will find it much harder to achieve than anything it has done until now.

One of the first barriers that needs to be overcome is the belief that humanity is already above nature. Only the achievement of peace can truly draw a line between humanity and everything else in the material world. Peace is the only collective coming-into-Being that exists, the only step that raises genuinely new possibilities for our species. Peace is about exploring the senses that lie dormant within us. Killing deprives everyone, it harms us all. Our fellow human beings are not unrelated, separate and remote. We are all part of the world and the substance of life collectively.

Efforts to identify this complex truth loom large in human history. At times, understanding has grown and become strong. Today, it is weak and fading. Enlightened ideas appear to be absurdities, because the smiling arrogance of science and technology have allowed soldiers and economists to define progress.

Human behaviour today is not the result of rational considerations, despite what people believe. It stems still from a passionate delight in animalistic destruction. Humanity has forgotten what it once understood better, the living substance buried within each of us that has the power to transcend everything. The world is not what is outside, as so many seem to believe. That is why they see only enemies, danger, fear and death. It is what is inside, the light of experience and perception, the flaring up of the divine, as Hermann Hesse so elegantly puts it, that matters. Only that can move humanity forward.

Every death in Ukraine and Russia is a repetition of humanity's failure to understand this. That is self-evident.

Well, those are my thoughts today. I'm seeing your brother next week and will write again when I get back.

Before I go, I also wanted to tell you about the Fosters. Do you remember them? Peter and Jeanette, both lawyers. He became a circuit judge a few years ago. At the beginning of December he was convicted for the murder of one of his assistants. She disappeared 15 years ago, with no trace ever found. I visited him in prison before I left for Asia. He says someone with a grudge against him had hacked into his laptop and left incriminating letters and manipulated images before tipping off the police. He said the evidence was so overwhelming that he was unable to build an effective defence.

As he said to me, who knows what's true any longer?

With love
Max

~

This article was inspired by Hermann Hesse's book, *If the War Goes On: Reflections on War and Politics*, 1946 edition.

CHAPTER 4

WHAT IS THIS THING CALLED THINKING?

Part 2: The Ethereal

Bonn na Cnoc, Àird nam Murchan
February 16

Dear nephew,

A few weeks ago I sent you my research notes on the physical process of what is called thinking. Enclosed are my thoughts on the more challenging topic of thinking itself, on the ethereal process of thinking.

Please send me your thoughts!

∾

2: Notes on the ethereal process of thinking

Based on my research so far, it is clear that the physical aspects of what we call thinking are poorly understood. It is also clear that what I have called the ethereal process of thinking has received very little serious analysis. What is it that calls on us to think? That is the question. What is this thing called thinking? Is what is *called* thinking the same as *actual* thinking?

The original word in Old English, *thinken*, has two meanings. It means "the appearance of (something)", and "to exercise the faculty of reason, to cogitate". It means "to say to one's self mentally".

Another meaning, "to seem", has been absorbed or lost, but remains in the word methinks, "it seems to me". Think and thank come from the same linguistic root in several European languages; German, Frisian, Saxon, Norse, English. To thank someone is to show you have thought about something they did.

What we call thinking cannot be traced from somewhere to somewhere else like a cart track. It is possible that the question on what is called thinking can never be definitively settled, now or ever.

Still, there is much that we can say about what thinking is, and is not. Thinking is not an accumulation of memories. Thinking is not simply the gathering of thoughts. Thinking does not exist in any single place. Thinking is enigmatic, and an act of solitude. We cannot enter someone else's mind and take their thoughts. Their thoughts are theirs alone, which is why thinking is a lonely process for each of us. What each of us conceives and asserts is not the same; the thoughts are not identical. How they differ, we do not know.

Differences in thinking create misunderstandings. Some thoughts are published or otherwise distributed, and these then occupy the minds of those who do not think. But a thought that takes occupation in another mind is not identical to the thought that was conceived.

A second point on which I am clear. We are in a world where there is a need for more thinking. There is not enough thinking, though this has always been so, since the beginning of time.

Still, today appears to be different. The nuclear, technological era of turbo-capitalism, with widening political and social divisions, calls for more thinking than before. A world of eight billion people calls for more thinking than before. While, in the past, humanity risked the collapse of the odd civilisation, today's threats have the potential to impact everyone. The risks are existential. The future of our species, and most others is at stake. It is now possible to make enormous errors within a few hours, or a few decades. The capacity for ill has been greatly augmented.

It seems to me that we can clearly say that there is not enough thinking on a large number of important issues: gender, immigration, democracy, war, freedom, international relations, weapons production, and many others. There is opinion but not thought. In many areas, thinking has become fossilised and unfocussed, so troubled and controversial that even to make this observation is to find oneself facing a populist wall of non-thought. Less controversial, perhaps, is thinking on climate change. It requires very little reflection to see there is not enough thinking on the topic of climate change.

You and I have talked about this many times.

Climate change can be addressed, as you have made clear in your books. The rate of increase of warming can be reduced and brought under control. Societies need to stop burning fossil fuels. The concentration of dangerous gases in the atmosphere can be reduced, to cut global temperatures, and regain equilibrium. But societies don't take the steps needed. They choose instead to fiddle around on the fringes, to create new business opportunities for electric cars, solar panels and windmills while all the time making the overall situation worse, and consciously. They know the consequences of what they are doing but they ignore them. The impact of climate change is visible and getting worse. Yet people do not change.

They are not thinking.

To any reasonable, thinking, person this makes no sense. It's like a man who smokes 40 cigarettes a day developing lung cancer and deciding to smoke even more. I'm sure the majority of people in the world don't want worsening climate change. Yet that is their destiny, and they know it.

The world is not thinking.

Let's approach the question differently. Why do we think? Do we think because it is useful or because we have no option, because it is harder *not* to think? If we say it is useful, what do we mean? Does it serve a purpose? Do dead ends exist in thought?

Thinking does not always promote practical wisdom, nor solve cosmic riddles. There is nothing, no salvation, to be found in thinking. It is simply something we are called to do. It is being human, and understanding where we belong, a search for truth, our individual attempts to reveal what is concealed. As Heidegger says, trying to define thinking to someone is like trying to describe colours to a blind person.

Thinking requires each of us to ask questions about the world as we perceive it, but without any clear sense of the destination, of where this takes us or why. It seems that it is enough simply to be on the path. Thinking also requires listening, and a rigour and strictness. It requires thoughts that are not systematic or conceptual. It is a search for answers. A Japanese sword maker strives to understand the metal he works, tries to understand the effects of heat and time, the hidden riches of nature, and the strength of his whole craft. It is not the chance for profit that draws him to his art but the chance of discovery. Thinking is much the same.

How should we distinguish between chatter and reflection, between those with sightless eyes and noise-cluttered ears, and fat floppy tongues, who do not regulate the uncontrolled contrasts in their thoughts? How should we open our minds, not resist the unfamiliar, or that which is inconvenient or challenges us? To do that we must listen and understand before we dismiss, not dismiss before we understand. Paradoxically perhaps, thinking requires us to embrace misunderstanding.

Does thinking change over time; does it evolve? Do today's Greeks think as the ancient Greeks? Do the Chinese think in the same way as their ancestors during the Sung Dynasty? Values have changed, and the language has evolved. But has thinking changed?

What provokes us to thought today? What do we call thought-provoking? The answer today is, I think, almost the same as it was for Heidegger a century ago. What provokes the most thought currently is everything that is dark, threatening and gloomy, all that is adverse. When we say that something is thought-provoking, we almost always mean something injurious, something negative.

Current thinking promotes every form of nothingness. It is nihilistic. People everywhere spend their days recording and tracking real or imagined decline. They spend their lives in fear, fretting about the threat of everything falling apart, worrying about war, and the imminent destruction of the world. Most so-called serious books, online posts, and news articles wallow in deterioration and depression while most others only offer trite empty-headed vacuity, bereft of intelligent thought. It is all so tiresome.

Why is there not enough thinking? Is it because what must be thought about turns people away, or because not enough people are able or willing to reach out to what must be thought?

Again, let's ask Heidegger for inspiration, and examine what he calls the problem of one-track thinking.

One-track thinking has nothing to do with rails or technology. Nor has it grown out of human laziness. One-track thinking is an unsuspected and inconspicuous phenomenon, in which the essence of technology and technocracy takes the lead. What do I mean? I mean people hear the message about economic growth and market liberalism but not the one about nature. When it comes to serious issues, people think about one thing at a time. They don't join them up. Almost all the problems of the world, from poverty to inequality, war and climate change, are interconnected. They are all part of the same problem. They are the result of too many power-hungry, selfish, competitive people living according to an economic system that is ecologically destructive by design, that feeds their material desires endlessly, that calls every damaging consequence an "externality", which it says should be ignored. That is *precisely* what modern economics says.

As you will see with my third set of notes, I have explored the way thinking is framed like this in more depth, looking in detail at that system of closed-minded thinking that is called modern economics.

The result of too little thinking is that the human world is not just out of kilter, it is tumbling towards useless oblivion. Nietzsche saw all this coming a century ago, of course. "The wasteland grows", he said.

What did he mean, exactly?

According to Heidegger, he meant "the *devastation* grows". What is growing, what is surrounding us like a black cloud, darkening the light, is more than simple destruction. It is unthinking devastation that is growing. Devastation is more unearthly than destruction. Devastation doesn't just threaten to sweep away all that has been achieved. It makes every recovery impossible. It blocks progress and prevents rebuilding. While destruction sweeps away even nothingness, devastation spreads everything that blocks and prevents.

This growing devastation can be mapped. It is palpable. Especially in the West, this devastation haunts everyone, everywhere in the most unearthly way. It is hidden in the slow sinking sands, in the accelerating expulsion of thought people are forced to endure as they watch the world evolve from the discomfort of their living room sofa.

People have lost their thinking in the constructed mire. They have sacrificed thinking to having views and opinions.

Having a view is not insignificant, of course. All our daily lives require it, and necessarily so.

But today's views are often dominated by notions of decline, and by those that glorify inhumanity and war, by ideas that anaesthetise sympathy. People have become too accustomed to thinking only about themselves, and seeing only false, ugly and horrible events around them, as if they live constantly in ghastly nightmares. There is not a trace of serenity and kindness in their eyes, not a hint of any gratitude for life, nor trust. The media continuously promotes jealous, conceited behaviour. It feeds negative and cynical perspectives, goads people to mock others and promote hatred. Why? Because the more provocative and controversial what is said, the better. The click-through revenue matters, not whether what's said is balanced, uplifting or even reasonable. Creating an emotional response is key, and the seeds of negative emotions are so much easier to fertilise.

There is very little interest in thinking, in a thinking response.

People say anything to receive attention, like neglected children. This makes the truth hard to identify. Opinions become polarised, binary, black and white, morally absolutist. Without grey, people can only be horrified or numbed by the endless flood of dogmatic one-sided statements. All this divides. It makes consensus and cooperation harder; it creates barriers to harmony that have to be first overcome before any better process can begin.

Another trend, just as concerning. The past is being erased. Academics are finding old papers are being deleted; historical data is being removed. So many of the research papers that are published are funded[1] by those who want a particular view to prevail,[2] who want to undermine academic consensus, block political action, or suppress vital information, even when it could save lives.[3]

If the results of academic research are likely to be unpopular, it is often not funded. The papers that *are* published — on plastic waste, vaccines, climate change, sensitive political issues, race, gender, and a hundred other topics that require our thinking — are often biased. They undermine thought. Data on climate change has been erased.[4]

1   Fabbri A, Lai A, Grundy Q, Bero LA. "The Influence of Industry Sponsorship on the Research Agenda: A Scoping Review". Am J Public Health. 2018 Nov;108(11):e9-e16. doi: 10.2105/AJPH.2018.304677. Epub 2018 Sep 25. PMID: 30252531; PMCID: PMC6187765.

2   Reproducibility and Research Integrity, House of Commons Select Committee Report, May 2023 https://publications.parliament.uk/pa/cm5803/cmselect/cmsctech/101/summary.html.

3   https://catalogofbias.org/biases/industry-sponsorship-bias/.

4   https://www.scientificamerican.com/article/climate-web-pages-erased-and-obscured-under-trump/.

Half of all medical trials are not published. Despite it being illegal in many countries, they remain hidden.[5]

Two small examples to illustrate this trend, though there countless more:

A study by the University of Oxford of 65 drug trials sponsored by makers of new drugs found there were favourable conclusions in 79% of them. In 30 studies where the trial was not sponsored by a drug maker, only 10% reported favourable results. The researchers concluded "the main factor associated with the results and conclusions of industry-sponsored research… is research sponsorship".[6]

A second study[7] found that when the results of drug trials for antidepressants were positive, 97% of them were published. When the results were negative or questionable, only 8% were published accurately. Nearly a third were published with "narrative spin" while 61% were not published at all.

All this scientific erasing and funnelling is just one example of how thinking is being consciously constrained.

The media is restricting thinking too. Information is being suppressed when it doesn't fit a particular narrative. During the Covid pandemic, Facebook labelled a peer-reviewed BMJ article as partly false just because "the authors did not express unreserved support for vaccination". Instagram "shadow-banned" another medical paper for false content, which Twitter, now X, wrongly tagged as misleading, even though it had won a major prize for good scientific communication.[8]

5   https://senseaboutscience.org/alltrials/.

6   Catalogue of Bias Collaboration, Holman B, Bero L, & Mintzes B. Industry Sponsorship bias. Catalogue Of Bias 2019: https://catalogofbias.org/biases/industry-sponsorship-bias/.

7   Erick, H et al, (2008) "Selective Publication of Antidepressant Trials and Its Influence on Apparent Efficacy", *New England Journal of Medicine* Volume 358, No 3. DOI: 10.1056/NEJMsa065779.

8   https://www.bmj.com/content/376/bmj.095.

Social media has played a pivotal role in polarising thinking on climate change, with a bias that one academic study said poses a serious challenge to society.[9]

Do you remember that shooting at the Comet Ping Pong[10] pizza restaurant a few years ago? It was caused by fake media posts, designed to stir trouble, intended to inspire unthinking violence.

Countless factually wrong statements are posted online every day, yet social media firms have stopped fact-checking. Doctored photographs, false data charts, and wrongly-attributed quotes are constantly being posted, deliberately designed to provoke outrage, to test people. At the same time, genuine news reports are often dismissed as fake.

All this means that sowing seeds of doubt has become easier. Those websites and self-righteous news organisations that publish "fact check" articles are some of the worst offenders here. They claim their version of the truth as the only truth, when it is really just another opinion.

Social media damages thinking in many other ways, of course, and this has been well documented. It reduces concentration, undermines reflection, cuts stored memory, changes perceptions of value, and reduces real-life interaction. All this influences thinking and the opportunity to think, mostly negatively. It's creating mental health problems[11] too, especially among young people.

All this is clever, as well as dystopian.

People's opinions are being carefully reprogrammed, to make them angry, or act in particular ways, to control their thinking. I have a lot

---

9   Modgil S, Singh RK, Gupta S, Dennehy D. "A Confirmation Bias View on Social Media Induced Polarisation During Covid-19". Inf Syst Front. 2021 Nov 20:1–25. doi: 10.1007/s10796-021-10222-9. Epub ahead of print. PMID: 34840520; PMCID: PMC8604707.

10   https://www.marubeni.com/en/research/potomac/backnumber/19.html.

11   Riehm KE, Feder KA, Tormohlen KN, et al. "Associations Between Time Spent Using Social Media and Internalizing and Externalizing Problems Among US Youth". JAMA Psychiatry. 2019;76(12):1266–1273. doi:10.1001/jamapsychiatry.2019.2325.

of research on this topic and will send you my notes separately. When thinking is manipulated deliberately, it is often hard to perceive because it is so enveloping, so all-encompassing. It becomes an interconnected system of thought, solitary confinement for the mind.

All the examples I've mentioned, the preference for provocative statements, the restrictions on scientific publishing, and the media's manipulation of the truth, is blocking, limiting, and channelling thinking.

It makes it harder for people to find a positive pathway. I will come back to this shortly.

Of course, it has always been hard to identify the truth. Manipulation of reality has always been done to restrict thinking and close pathways. The difference now is that misinformation is more widespread and disparate. It is done by so many people and organisations, and for so many different reasons. Identifying the truth has become harder, which means it is harder to think clearly and objectively. The internet and social media, developments that were meant to set insight and information free, to release people from the shackles of untruth, has made the problem much worse.

"The time of the most despicable man is coming, he that is no longer able to despise himself."[12]

Especially in the West, thinking has been levelled and flattened, framed within one elevation. Most people view the world in a near-identical way, without a clear understanding that their overarching picture of reality is not the only view.

Western media and education systems have built this unified way of thinking with care. The structure has architects, people who designed the frame and filled the spaces, who chose the colours. They constructed this way of thinking deliberately, so that everything in the West that is called progress has been carefully shaped to fit inside one thought box, everything is locked within a growth-focussed,

---

12   Nietzsche, F, *Thus Spoke Zarathrustra.*

science-based, free-market liberal, hatred of any alternative, there is no God, prison.

All is carefully designed platitude.

I have explored this process in considerable detail in my third set of notes, this manufactured worldview, which I have called "the currency of thought". It has a pernicious history that goes back centuries: boxed-in Western thinking has passed through several major iterations.

∿

A different way to think about thinking is to consider what should not be called thinking.

What should not be called thinking?

Thinking is not simply having an opinion, or a notion. It is not just having an idea. It is not a representation of something, or a perspective on a state of affairs. Thinking is not a chain of premises leading to a conclusion. Thinking is not conceptual or systematic. All these concepts are useful to understand thinking, but they are not what thinking is.

Thinking is made harder to understand because so many preconceptions stand in the way. To learn thinking is like learning a new language, Heidegger says. It is necessary to forget the one we already know.

In thinking about thinking, he says the process is too often equated with logic.[13] Those who try to understand thinking often try to define it scientifically. This leads to the notion that our behaviour, opinions, and actions are determined by some sequential process of thought, through logical steps that are taken inside our minds. It is the approach of the "rational conscience" I mentioned earlier, the approach of the rational being. It is Aristotle's idea of the rational soul.

---

13   *Was heißt Denken*, Part 1, Lecture II, third page.

Heidegger says this approach to thinking is favoured for another reason. It is preferred because it yields an assured profit for those wanting to construct a technological universe.

If thinking can be explained by science, if it is something logical, then a computer can be taught to think. This makes it possible to create artificial intelligence. The flaw, of course, is that thinking requires consciousness, and scientists have no idea what that is, or how to define it.

Still, this approach to understanding thinking, this assumption that thought is logical, that the mind is a machine, encourages people to believe technology can solve almost every problem. If thinking is logical, a machine will be able to 'think' better than people. It can be better and also Be. This idea reinforces a vital element of what is *called* modern thinking, as opposed to what modern thinking really is. It extracts one area of understanding, one way to see the world, the scientific way, and extrapolates it to encompass everything, to view the world through this one small lens.

This mindset, this pathway to what is called thinking, is deeply embedded, especially in the West. It is a pillar of what is called Western thought.

Because people believe the world is rational, logical and scientific, because they think it is a machine that can be regulated, they think technology can fix enormous, interconnected and hugely complex problems such as species loss and climate change. There is no need to constrain the rate of population growth, no need to abandon the focus on economic expansion, no need to limit personal freedom, no need to try and live in harmony with the world. Everything becomes a technological problem. Everything can, and will be understood by science, by logic. Anything not yet understood should only be examined through this one eyeglass. The world is a machine. Human beings are machines. Reality is scientific, rational. All this thinking is built on the notion of logical thought.

The flaw here, of course, is that the world is not rational. Human behaviour is not rational. Thinking is not rational. Reality is not rational.

This science-based, logic-framed way to thinking funnels understanding. It promotes the idea that human development is unidirectional, that humanity is on a steady upward path of discovery, invention and progress. Every technological development, every new product, every piece of research, is hailed as good and useful without much thought, without asking whether or not this is really true.

Unfortunately, such thinking can only lead to disappointment, because reality will eventually be revealed.

Like modern economics, the thinking system of science occupies far too great a space in the modern Western mind, far more than it should. It is viewed as something of the highest order. It is ranked higher than traditional views that see science as just one aspect of human civilisation. It attempts to push almost *all* thinking through the same narrow tube of ideas, to force people to adopt one approach. It is like the thinking of the Church before the Enlightenment.

At its core, technology is anything but human and yet this thought pillar of modern existence underpins the structure of almost everything. It defines contemporary reality. It denies the existence of anything that cannot be understood through scientific thought. It disregards the notion of any higher consciousness, or any universal realm, because such an idea cannot be validated by the methods it prescribes, it demands.

Nature, the world around us, is not a logical machine either and it cannot be fully understood through science and technology, yet scientists expect us to think it can.

Richard Dawkins, that British arch-science proponent, the man for whom there is definitively no God, whose popular profile is built on statements designed to shock (your aunt laughs when I say this), has concerns about children reading fairy tales.[14] He worries the ideas they contain make it hard for them to develop a scientific mind.

To me, this is a perfect example of the closed-headedness of many scientists. He's saying, in effect, that stories which encourage children to imagine, to wonder, to ask questions about reality and what's possible are not useful. Does he want scientists without creative abilities, without any understanding of allegory? Stories about magic, unreal worlds and other dimensions are surely what science needs. Is the ability to imagine not essential?

Let me put the question about scientific thinking another way. Does science help humanity move forward positively?

In some ways, the answer is obviously yes. Science could make it possible for people to live better lives and work less. It can cure diseases and help people live longer.

But if the rewards of new technologies are unfairly distributed, so most people have to work just as much as they did before, or a new technology means there is not enough work for people to earn what they need to live, and medicines are being developed to help cure diseases that have been caused by other technical innovations, by chemically laden foods, in an effort to profit on both sides, or science is used to spy on people and make weapons, how does all this help humanity move forward positively? How does science help people live in peace, with respect for one another, with tolerance, and in harmony? Achieving peace has nothing to do with science or a laboratory. It has nothing to do with logic. It comes from thinking, from imagining how such a state can be achieved, from identifying the conditions necessary, and then working to create these. Technology doesn't help.

Don't we all have a yearning for something better, for a higher level of human attainment, and sensible leaders to guide us? As we stare from the window, don't we all dream about another, more beautiful, life, where there is no jealousy, where common sense and good order

---

14   https://theweek.com/uk-news/58836/richard-dawkins-fairy-tales-are-bad-for-children.

prevail, where people can trust one another, treat them with respect, with cheerfulness and consideration? Should life not be a pleasure, with the joy found in the simple living of it, as Tolstoy says at the end of his book *War and Peace*? Can't humanity be beneficial to nature, and honour the unity of all things? Don't people benefit from understanding literature, music, and art? Doesn't everyone dream of more than the plasticine imitation, laboratory-manufactured, pale shadow of life that most people lead today? So many live in gloom, in fear of poverty, sorrow and death, under the light of demons, and yet they still kill each other in droves. What mishap has caused such a life on this planet? It is all so ridiculous and foolish, so disturbing in a shameful way. It does not have to be like this. Humanity can choose something better, if we think.

∾

Another example of closed-minded thought in the West are common perspectives on Chinese medicine.

Chinese medicine is often dismissed in the West. It is not regarded as scientific, despite hundreds of millions of people trusting it every day, and their ancestors trusting it for centuries. If it didn't work, the practitioners would surely have been dismissed as charlatans long ago.

As you know, I've benefited from Chinese medicine myself many times.

Unlike in the West, where everyone is considered the same sort of machine, patients in China are treated as individuals. Doctors ask different questions from those in the West, about heat and dampness, for example. They assess the flow of energy through the body. They examine the tongue and take the pulse from both wrists, for they are not the same.

Of course, there are many conditions Chinese medicine can't treat. But there are many it can, and often more effectively and less harmfully than Western medicine. Yet Western science denies the efficacy. It is another example of closed-minded thinking.

A personal example, you may recall. I suffered from high blood pressure a few years ago. After trying all sorts of medicines prescribed by Western doctors who took no interest in wanting to identify the source of the problem, and having suffered from all sorts of unpleasant side effects from the tablets they prescribed, I went to a Chinese doctor. Within weeks of taking her medicine, things began to improve. The most shocking outcome though was when I went back to the Western doctor and told him I no longer needed his tablets. He measured my blood pressure, found it acceptable, and smiled. I mentioned I had been taking Chinese medicine but he never asked me about it, not one question. His mind was closed, only interested in what his own science told him. He had no desire to know how another cure might work. I told two friends who are doctors about it too, and the same thing happened. They showed no interest in how the Chinese medicine had worked, or even asked what it was. It made me think. What are they training doctors to do these days? What are they training doctors to think?

The Chinese approach to medicine means people in China think differently to those in the West in other ways. For example, there is a major shortage of donated blood in China, and a large trade in illegal blood as a result. Until 1998, so few people gave blood, they had to be paid.[15] Since then, in an effort to persuade people to donate, they are offered gifts, as well as several days off work, and a nutrition allowance. Donors get priority access to transfusions if they ever need one. Even so, donations are around a fifth of the level in the West.

This reluctance to give blood is not down to a fear of infection, a mistrust of doctors, or the inconvenience, though these factors do play a small role.

Traditional Chinese medicine considers blood of vital importance to the body, and any sudden loss is thought harmful.[16] According to

15   https://doi.org/10.1016/j.tmrv.2016.11.001.

16   https://doi.org/10.1177/21582440231152404.

Confucian thinking, our physical existence, our bodies, including our blood, skin and hair, are granted by our parents. To love and protect the body is to love and respect one's parents. Damaging the body, even by giving blood, can be viewed as an impiety. So people considering donating blood generally ask their parents' permission, because it is their parents who gave them life.

Donating blood is thought to lead to reduced immunity and a loss of vitality, or *yuán qì* (元氣) in Chinese. In Japanese this is called *genki* (元気), health and energy.

The concept of *yuán qì* dates back more than 2,000 years. It is the essential life energy, the constitution people are born with. It contains the vital potential in every person, which is gradually used up in the course of life. *Yuán qì* can be conserved but never replenished.

Blood is viewed as a yin substance (as opposed to a yang substance) that nourishes and moistens the body. It provides the foundation for consciousness. The Chinese say blood "houses the mind". Healthy blood is vital to clear thinking, good memory, good mental health, and good sleep. Blood keeps the eyes moist and bright. For women, the reproductive cycle depends on healthy blood.

This thinking makes it is easy to understand why blood is not something people are willing to donate, even in a culture where benevolence, caring and helping others is important. When someone needs blood, it is often donated by their relatives.

The Japanese, and others in Asia, believe a person's blood defines their personality. In Japan this is called Ketsueki-gata. Even to Western science, this idea is not as strange as it might initially appear. Western science acknowledges different blood types have different characteristics.

Could blood types affect personality? Could they determine thinking?

People with blood type A are much less attractive to mosquitoes but they carry a higher risk of heart disease and a much higher risk of stomach cancer than blood types O and B. Type B has 50,000 times more strains of friendly bacteria than types A and O. People with type O have a lower risk of pancreatic cancer and dying from malaria, though they are more likely to get ulcers, and have a higher risk of rupturing an Achilles tendon.

According to the Japanese, people with blood type A are creative, sensible and patient, but also stubborn and tense. Type B people are passionate, active and strong, though selfish, unforgiving, and erratic. AB people are controlled, rational, and adaptable but indecisive, forgetful, and irresponsible. Type O people are strong-willed and intuitive but also cold and unpredictable.

Western science says this is all nonsense. It dismisses Chinese and Japanese ways of thinking about blood as superstition or pseudoscience. Yet hundreds of millions of people in Asia and other parts of the world disagree. Ironically perhaps, Aristotle and Hippocrates also believed there was a link between personality and blood.[17]

Because Western science defines the parameters of what is accepted as science itself, its thinking is tautological. To require or demand scientific proof of absolutely everything around us is to shut out almost everything that is not yet understood. A proof of everything is not just impossible. It is also unnecessary, inappropriate and undesirable. Many of the things that matter cannot be objectively, logically, explained.

Restricting thinking to what is called logical thinking is not logical thinking.

Science also provides an excellent illustration of Heidegger's notion of one-sided thinking. It explores elements, not the whole. It attempts to understand a period in time, without trying to understand history, because it cannot do so, scientifically. History cannot be understood through mathematics or logic, any more than a quadratic equation can explain our emotions.

---

17 Høyersten, J. G. (1997). "From Homer to Pinel: The concept of personality from antiquity until 1800 AD". *Nordic Journal of Psychiatry*, 51(5), 385-394. https://doi.org/10.3109/08039489709090734.

There's a short story by Hermann Hesse called "A Dream About the Gods". In it, a man approaches a large stone building full of light and finds it is the Temple of Knowledge. Inside the "Priests of Science" are talking to a large group of people. They are explaining how in the past people believed in Gods; in the Gods of War, Love, Thunder, and so on. Many in the audience laugh. Now, say the priests, thanks to science, people know better. Then the sky darkens and a cold wind blows. Lightening strikes and the people run from the temple in fear, trampling over the narrator. When he recovers, he staggers outside and finds the city in flames. The clouds above him slowly part and several great figures step forward into the world. It is the Gods who were banished by science.

Gods don't have to be real to influence thought, to change how people see the world, or how they behave. An allegorical God has value too.

The beating heart of history, poetry, art, language, nature, human behaviour and God remain completely outside the realm of what is called science, far from its weak grasp, for it has no mechanism to approach them. These elements of existence lie at our core and yet science has no access to them because it is not thinking.

Scientists have cajoled, pushed, and shoved us all into a box of unitary thought. The sciences are necessary, but their limits need to be remembered. Our minds have views on everything. But when people are told to look at only one side of everything, and told to forget that it is only one side, they lose sight of the other sides. Truth is diminished.

∽

Let's ask the question another way: what causes thinking? Or does this take us back to the start? Is what is called thinking, what calls on us to think, the same as asking what causes us to think?

When it comes to thinking about thinking, Heidegger says we should take care not to form opinions too quickly, to pigeonhole everything in a flash. We will "need bothersome detours and crutches" to understand, he says, and these will cause us to "run counter to what we expect".[18] But then, if there is not enough thinking, running counter to what we expect is perhaps what is needed.

What if the pathway to understanding thinking is unpleasant, or it seems hopeless or superfluous? If we think it foolish to think about what is called thinking, is it better to remain outside? Perhaps. Thinking is not a universal requirement. It is not for everyone.

How much of what is called thinking is tied to what is called Being?

Immediately we run into a problem, certainly if we think about this word in English. In English, the meaning of being is relatively simple: "a living thing". That is far short of what we mean. The German word, *Dasein*, is more what we need.

Being is something that is conceivable, and so capable of existing. It is the essence of a thing. Being is that which constitutes existence. This is why I added a capital "B". I want to show that I mean more than a living thing, a mere personality.

As I write in English, understanding this idea may need further explanation. What do the Greeks say about Being? Can that improve our understanding of the concept? Parmenides says, "One should both say and think that Being is."

Okay. But that's simple. What else can be thought or said about Being? Only that "it is". Being is. Saying "it is" tells us everything and nothing. It speaks nothing of the existence or essence of what we mean by Being.

What is this thing called Being? Is it thought?

Is Being thought? Is Being the answer to the central question we are trying to explore? Let's be bold. Are thinking and Being the same thing? Is thinking the only concrete proof of our existence, the proof of our Being? Kant says Being is one of the most un-analysable of concepts. If this is true, and Being is thinking, then it must be equally impossible to analyse thinking. Understanding thinking would be an

---

18   *Was heißt Denken*, Part II, Lecture V, last paragraph.

attempt to understand Being. The process "offers no way out", said Aristotle.

Are we confusing Being with awareness? Descartes' first principle was "I think therefore I am". When he says "I am", does he mean Being? It doesn't seem quite the same.

"I think therefore I exist." Is that what he means? Existing and thinking are not the same. A car exists, but it does not think.

The sentence could also be: "I am aware and therefore I exist." I am aware that I exist. Is awareness the same as thinking? Pushkin is aware he exists. He understands pleasure and pain. He pats my face gently with his paw to wake me when he needs to go out during the night. The squirrels and birds in the garden are aware they exist. They know desire. They have memory. They make judgements and evaluations. The birds know when they are to be fed. They take turns at the feeder. They understand time, not sunlight. The days shorten and lengthen yet some come to feed at exactly the same time each day. The squirrels pause and consider before they leap, to raid the bird feeder. We move it. They recalculate. They make judgements. They learn what works and what doesn't. Are they not thinking? Does this not show they are self-aware? Pushkin is most certainly self-aware!

I believe Heiddeger is slightly mistaken here. He says animals do not think because they never "confront" anything. He says this shows they do not perceive themselves; they do not perceive themselves because they cannot speak. Yet animals confront the world all the time. They confront a threat. They confront your aunt when she goes out to feed them. They get closer to her, as they become familiar with her. We must not assume these other creatures do not speak just because we do not understand their language. That is the one-sided thinking of science.

Is a tree aware it exists? Can it think? Is thinking a different level of consciousness from awareness? What did Descartes really want to say here? He writes of existence. Is awareness of our existence all we can be sure of? An imbecile can be aware of his existence. But does he think? Does he understand that everything around him is ambiguous?

$$\sim$$

What else can we ask that might help us understand what is called thinking? What do we need to avoid?

And here we have an answer. If everything that is thought-provoking is calling us to think, let us not be the "last man", says Nietzsche. Let us not be the generation that does not think, which is what he means, when there is so much that needs to be thought about. We seem to be in grave danger of not thinking enough, of making everything small.

"The earth has become smaller, and on it hops the last man who makes everything small."[19]

Humanity does not appear able to rise up to the task today. *We have invented happiness, say the last men, the ones who are not up to the task.* People need to learn to listen with their eyes, to understand beauty again. The world is becoming more thought-provoking and yet our nature is undetermined. Humans are told they are rational animals, trained to be rational. This is a misunderstanding. They are not yet brought to their full nature because they still think they are rational animals. We need to be carried beyond ourselves and yet we appear unwilling to *despise what is so despicable*, to overcome our current nature and find a bridge to our real nature, a better path.

This does not mean casting off into the ocean unsupported, without a plan. We must first learn to Be, be rendered capable of Being, fitting servants of the earth. That will not come by wielding high-purpose powers, or through a technological transformation of the planet. That is not thinking. It will not come from an unbridled imagination, particularly if that is degenerate. It will not come by us pushing those who are shallow and misconceived into power, to be the top functionaries in government and international organisations. It will not come by

---

19 Nietzsche, F, *Thus Spoke Zarathrustra.*

us idly dreaming about a coming "superman", someone who will lead humankind towards some ill-defined paradise. All this risks taking us headlong into the void.

Humanity needs people of action, yes. But it first needs people of thought. Almost all of today's public figures, almost all those who sit in the limelight, are about as far from supermen and superwomen as is humanly possible. I cannot identify any candidate to be one of Nietzsche's "supermen" in the West at all.

What counts for action today, international gatherings and associations, conventions and agreements never gets beyond talk and empty declarations, lavishly signed. Those who attend these gatherings make plenty of proposals on what should be done. What is interesting though, what needs thought, is too often reduced to the indifferent and boring.

Most us are left to hide in the wasteland within. We allow others to think for us, and the rhythm of history to decide our fate. Before the Enlightenment it was the Church that controlled thinking for most people. Then it became science, politicians, the media. Now it is economics. It is economists who tell us what to think, what to believe, what to get angry about, what to celebrate. They tell us *how* to celebrate, *how* to weep, what to care about, an endless stream of empty thoughts fed to us, to keep us docile. It has become ever-simpler, all this coercing, coaxing and threatening.

At one time this perspective on thinking was not held in the West; it is still not held elsewhere. Thinking was, and still can be, a pathway built on that moving ocean that is impossible to anticipate.

Can we find the path to better thinking, even if we start from a great distance away? Is there some bright ray of hope that we can shine into that obfuscation which so depresses the world and that lighter-than-air nothingness that fills so many minds, by design? Can we gather thoughts that please us, that take us forward positively? Is there some way of thinking that does not oppress us, that can be dragged in by force?

How can we melt the frozen wasteland? What thoughts are there for joyful things, beauty, graciousness, and kindness? Are these ideas to be left to our individual feelings and experiences, blown from the winds of collective thought? What of the mysterious, and those things that offer real food for thought? Where are the ideas that offset this malice-soaked evil that is fed to us?

It is there, if we look, if we take a different route. We all know that. If we look in another way, just for a moment, in another direction, we can all see there is a different path ahead. This should be our highest concern. We first need to understand that there is a need to move ahead differently, and think freshly, but not dismiss so much of the past that we lose good thought.

Modern thinking also dismisses the work of past thinkers too easily, those like Parmenides or Heraclitus. These men, and so many others, should not be considered museum pieces of intellectual history, past souls to be placed on display for scholarship, their thoughts frozen or forgotten. There is plenty of good thought in human history that can be gathered and built on. The way that is left behind us, past thought, does not need to remain there. It can help us build the next step, and project us forward. At the same time, we must take care not to let the past lead us unthinkingly. We should take care not to adopt traditional thinking just because it is traditional. That risks making us prisoners of a past destiny. Traditions are full of self-deceptions to entangle us and block thinking, that prevent us from hearing and seeing good alternatives.

In any case, we must break free, those of us in the West. We need to reject what has failed but also understand that a haughty contempt for all that has been will not help us either. It will take more effort, more thought, to escape the uniform one-sidedness that boxes us in.

Thinking about thinking today is to think about this process, to begin that journey across an ever-changing landscape where it is impossible to take a firm hold, but where there can be hope if we seek it out. It is an adventure into the unknown, a search for the essence of truth, the essence of beauty, the essence of grace. We need to turn away from all this melancholy and despair, stop drifting blindly. We need to shake the foundations of thinking until the last century appears as the tragic chapter of a poorly conceived story. This necessary shaking of the foundations does not necessarily mean revolution and collapse, though it might. What's needed is the search for a new equilibrium, a position of rest that has not been achieved because that place is at the heart of the shock that lies ahead. Today, humanity lags curiously behind.

Humanity's thinking, especially in the West, is falling far short of what is needed. It is not capable of wisely confronting the coming challenges, the historical shape of which we can already glimpse, that concern our fate on Earth. All those things that are undecided stand out clearly and even here the danger is that there is no decision, that these matters which must be decided are pushed aside because those who claim to think about them are not thinking. Their thoughts are too narrow and faint-hearted, deprived as they are of consideration and proper reflection. We have mislaid the instinct to see this, to fix our thinking.

One reason humanity lags behind is that our nature is still not fully developed, as I have already said. Our future is not assured today because rationality, this love of science and logic, still trumps sound thought. It trumps reason. There is unity in both, not in one alone. Reason says humanity needs to discard the boundless, purely quantitative striving for non-stop progress. Rationality says otherwise. It negates a quieter, more self-sacrificing way, where decisions are made carefully and speech is economical.

Today's one-sided way of thinking will be hard to change. This view, this blindness, which ignores reality and the essence of things, has puffed itself up to appear many-sided. It has been masked to appear harmless and neutral. This one-sided view, this flat, surface-deep perspective that thinks it deals with everything reduces all to the so-called precisions of the technological process by its uniformity and mindlessness.

Science no longer recognises sunrises and sunsets because it has unequivocally shown us that they are an illusion of the senses. And yet we still await the rising of the sun with a quickening pulse and a sense of beauty in our hearts, even when we have experienced it hundreds of times before. I believe it is that sense of beauty and anticipation that needs to be recaptured, to lead us forward.

We need to listen more carefully, and open our eyes, to hear the call to break free.

∾

My dear nephew,

That was a heavy meal for you to digest. Let me know when you are ready for me to send you more. I don't want to overwhelm you.

I am now researching the two other approaches to understanding thinking I mentioned: what I have called the currency of thinking, and how language impacts thought.

I am sending you what I have for now and will write again soon.

With love
Max

CHAPTER 5

ON LOVE

Zur frohen Aussicht, Zürich
April 17

Dear nephew,

Your aunt read my notes, and when she came to the sections on the thinking of science, where I say scientific thought has little useful to say about anything that's really important, she said I should give an example. She suggested I write about love.

So, here are my notes on love. It's a difficult subject, as hard as writing about thinking.

There are far more questions than answers.

~

How does science help us understand love? It can measure heartbeats, and describe the way people blush. It can faintly measure the melancholy after love has gone, and prescribe some tablets. But does science offer us any real guidance? How does it help us understand the essence of love, this core of life, this rumoured sixth sense? What insight can it give us to understand love's meaning and purpose? Where does love appear in the periodic table? Where is this vital element? Somewhere near oxygen, the breath of life, perhaps? It's not there. A trivial oversight. Perhaps love is a compound. A few milligrams of actinium, a pinch of gladolinium, and some ground antimony? It doesn't look a likely recipe.

Maybe the science of physics can help us? Is love the building block of every quark? Is it the God particle perhaps? Or maybe it's dark matter? None seems likely either.

What of mathematics? What number is love?

It tells us zero.

Better, then, to seek our answers elsewhere. One must tackle the question of love more broadly, and far more deeply than the superficiality of science can. We must turn to other sources for insight. What do music, poetry, and literature tell us?

They tell us love is a mystery.

Where it comes from, where it goes,
and how it passes, no one knows.

They tell us that sometimes love comes all at once, or never comes at all. Sometimes love is un-doubting, glad as a bright dawn. Sometimes it smoulders like the ashes of a fire. Sometimes it blossoms when autumn has begun, or withers anxiously to dust. Sometimes, it wends its way inside, like a snake, or slides carelessly away. Whoever is bold enough to grasp this serpent firmly can find it crushes the heart.

Love brings grief and black despair,
that's love's gift, it's everywhere.

Now we are getting somewhere. What else?

Love has no understanding of time, nor place. It has no laws. Love grants no human rights. It demands instead the right to everything, the whole of us. It has the power to overcome any resistance we muster, though it does not always use its advantage. Love is enigmatic.

It is not possible to doubt love, to ignore it, or outwit it. It is clever. It does not always take the same path. It takes possession without asking, like a fever. It clutches the heart, claws and scrapes at the mind. Like a hawk, it picks its prey. It captures and ensnares. There is no freedom for the soul when love takes a grip. It enslaves.

We know too that love always wins, even when it's lost. It advances life and ends it, like hunger. It can destroy us, or bring us nothing, and yet it is still called love. Love can unite and love can divide. It can offer no enjoyment. It can be self-sacrifice and death. It is ecstasy and pain. Love is truth and love is lies. Love is a conscience that consumes our every thought, as powerful as grief. Is that love too?

Love wipes self-control, outer calm, and common sense away. It evaporates without attention. It is entropic.

Natasha bent her head forward and blushed. "What happens to old love in a strong heart, love that's already dead?", she asked. "What happens when it still holds its place?"

"Only another love can drive it out", he answered.

Still, there's a need for more research. There are questions still unanswered.

How can love sometimes come so fast? How does the presence of another person quieten this raging tremor? Perhaps love is not a feeling at all. Maybe it's a malignancy, a malady, a certain condition of the body and soul.

What of the love of God, the love of a mother, love for country, the love I have for the small bird that pecks seed from my hand each morning, the love we all have for the gurgling chatter of a small stream? They all lazily embrace the same small word, and yet their meaning is as different as it possibly can be. Or is it?

Why does the chance for love not always come? Why is being loved not the same as giving it? Why are some unable to love? What blocks their love, what keeps it sealed?

Do other species love?

Of course they do. Watch them grieve. Or spend five minutes with a newborn lamb, and feel how it clings so tightly, how it gazes so trustingly into your eyes, how it gives itself unquestioningly. Watch how it and its mother embrace themselves in an unseen envelope of love. Other creatures love just the same as us. They tap the same font.

Science does not see this. It does not make observations with an open heart.

What of endurance? We know love is stronger than death. It can burrow into the lives of those remaining far more deeply than it ever did before. Does love outlast everything?

Which leads neatly to the hardest question of all.

Is love *actually* the soul? It's an unspeakably precious idea.

∾

CHAPTER 6

WHAT IS THIS THING CALLED THINKING?

Part 3: The Currency of Thinking

Johann Strauss Gasse, Wieden
Juni 8

Dear nephew,

Attached are my research notes on the third of the four topics on what is called thinking, on the currency of thinking. Some conclusions are not fully developed, and need a little work.

Is it not fascinating how Western minds have been shaped by systems of thought that are designed to constrain them, limit their freedom, and channel their thinking? Few people seem to be aware of how much their worldview is boxed in, how their minds have been manipulated. It's hard for them to stand far enough back, I suppose, to see their minds have been herded into a way of thinking that embraces and focusses everything unconsciously.

I look forward to your thoughts.

With much love
Max

~

The Currency of Thinking

What do I mean by the currency of thinking? I mean the framing that boxes in people's thoughts. I mean the mechanisms, the architecture, the operating system, through which thinking is deliberately or necessarily channelled, the containment that encloses nearly all thought. It is a human construct, this enclosure. It's a construction that is hard to perceive and even harder to break out from. It is a prison in which thinking is trapped, forced into a life sentence without understanding.

To explain this better, I've examined three thought currencies in Western European history: the thought currency of the Church, the currency of science, and today's thought currency of economics. All are boxed-in, constructed worldviews.

I'll start with the oldest, where traditional values were cleverly inverted, so that one group could take power from another, and transform the structure of society.

Like the other two thought currencies, the framework of thinking created by the Christian Church is a complete system, a *whole* view of the world, with all the elements tied together, each part a strand of an interconnected mesh.

1 — The Thinking Currency of the Church

Before I begin, there's something important I need to say. When I talk about the Christian Church and the mindset it created, I am not talking about faith or belief. I am talking about the organisation of the Catholic and Christian Churches, about the thinking they built. I am not talking about God, or any universal consciousness. It is the Church that developed the thinking system which boxed in thought for many centuries, which took power from the monarchies, as many other people have identified. I am not the first to explore this idea. Nietzsche writes about it in detail in *The Genealogy of Morals*.

My research, and everything I have learnt as I get older, has taught me that there is much more to the world, and to the universe, than modern science and our thoughts can explain. What that is, I don't know. I believe much of it is impossible to know, to understand. It is on a scale and across dimensions that is far beyond human ken, and probably always will be. To a large extent, that is what my work here is trying to explore. Personally, I have belief, I have a faith, though it does not fit well with the thought system created by the Church. I believe in a living world, with its own intelligence and momentum, something so vast that humanity cannot even imagine it, something beyond language. In the notes that follow I mean no offence to those who believe in any other God, or any other theory.

∽

Following the decline of the Roman Empire until the end of the Dark Ages, European society was mostly led by an aristocracy. It was ruled by kings, lords, and knights who typically owned those who lived on their lands. These people controlled the wealth, with their morality a triumphant affirmation of their own desires. These beasts of prey, always avidly rampant for spoils and victory, proud of their audacious barbarism, rejoiced in their imperishable memories of war, their delight in destruction.

The Church sat on the fringes. Its monasteries and convents were remote, its priests, monks and nuns devoted to prayer, self-sufficiency, and study. This society was relatively closed, with little or no uniformity, because most of the monasteries and convents followed the rules of individual abbots and mothers superior. There were many pilgrims, who travelled widely, even in the 6th and 7th centuries, seeking out these remote holy places, and the comfort of relics.

In writing this, I am reminded of the small town of North Berwick, near Edinburgh, where I went as a child. As well as several good golf courses, which is why my father took us, there are many wonderful sandy beaches. I loved the bracing walks, at least when it wasn't raining.

At the shore, near what is now a seabird centre, there is a chapel, the last remnant of an ancient church. As early as the 9th century, it was a gathering place for pilgrims who arrived from all over Europe. They would take a ferry, with nuns pulling on the oars apparently, out to the Isle of May, eight kilometres into the blustery estuary, at the mouth of the North Sea. On the island was another church, which became a Benedictine monastery a few centuries later. From there, they would catch a second ferry to Anstruther or Earlsferry, another eight kilometres away, before travelling on to St. Andrews, where there were important holy sites. I find it amazing that people travelled so far in those days, and took such dangerous journeys. The sea off the coast of North Berwick is not for the faint-hearted, even in summer. That people knew of such distant places, and had such sophisticated transport networks is fascinating.

Over the course of many centuries, this state of affairs slowly changed. Benedict of Nursia wrote some guiding principles which standardised the church's customs, better meeting the day-to-day needs of monks. This led to the rise of the Benedictine Order, and greater integration. Ireland became one of the truly great centres of monastic life, before other lands were gradually converted, including Scotland, parts of Germany, Switzerland, and today's northern France. The monks in these countries then took their faith to Poland, Hungary, Scandinavia, and elsewhere.

The Church continued to place a heavy emphasis on learning. Many monasteries became important hubs for education, agriculture and economic development, and through these they gradually acquired wealth, influence, and prestige, with abbots granted royal favours and political rights.

In the year 910, the abbots were formally united under the control of the Pope. This was an important step because it greatly reduced the influence of the kings and feudal lords over them.

Over the following centuries, the power of the Church continued to grow. It took control of the institution of marriage, and started to direct the activities of the aristocracy through crusades and by sanctioning their personal relationships. Cathedrals were built, vast otherworldly structures that increased the Church's power by directing people's minds towards a God who controls everything, who creates and destroys, who has far more power than any mortal king. Some cathedrals created schools to educate children, and art galleries to bring new thinking to adults. Bologna, and then Paris and Oxford, started universities. In the 11th century, in 1054, the Western branch of Christianity broke away from the Eastern branch, creating the Catholic Church.

All these developments increased the influence of the Church in the minds of the masses. The Church became a direct challenge to the power of the monarchies. As tensions rose, and without swords, soldiers and lances, the Church had to find a way to win this standoff in a way that did not involve direct physical conflict.

To do this, it created a system of thinking that cleverly inverted reality. It propagated a worldview that greatly weakened the influence of the feudal lords and kings, and made the Church all-powerful.

In the style of Sun Tzu, the ancient Chinese military strategist, the Church's system of thinking turned strengths into weaknesses and weaknesses into strengths. It flipped the traditional power structure. Being poor became good while being rich was equated to violence, Godlessness and lust. Poverty and weakness led to saintliness. Being sick, loathsome, and lowly was worthy. The oppressed became the pious, who deserved to be blessed, while the nobles and lords became symbols of covetousness and greed. Those who did not believe any of this, who opposed the Church, became the cursed and the damned. A terrible afterlife awaited them.

Those pagan traditions that had survived Roman persecution were cleverly assimilated to drive people away from Gods of nature. People were told to believe that the world and humankind had been created by one God, and that this God had a child with a mortal woman. God demanded that people work hard, and adopt a different form of morality and justice from the past to break from the morality of the aristocracy. People should fear the end of the world. People should fear what happens when they die. They should obey the laws of this God, handed down through priests and the Church. Only then could they avoid God's wrath.

Under the domain of the Church, people's lives became constrained. Everyone's day-to-day existence was dominated by concerns and obligations. Their sex lives were restricted, redesigned for utility alone. This God expected his disciples to drink his blood, and eat his flesh, in a process called transubstantiation. Believers were expected to offer prayers for miracles. Those who respected this God, who obeyed his teachings and set an example to others, had the chance to become saints, long after they died. Older ideas, a belief in the Earth and heavens, and ancient Gods were to be forgotten. The fertility days and carnival days of old became holy days, holidays.

The winter solstice became Christmas Day (according to the Julian calendar). A day to mark the Roman god of fertility, which involved feasting, carnal activities, and drinking, became the last feast before people were expected to fast for 40 days during Lent. The traditional festival marking the spring equinox, which had a hare as its symbol, became Easter. The Goddess of pagan traditions representing the mother became the Virgin Mary. Brigid, the Celtic Goddess associated with fertility and healing, became Saint Brigid of Ireland. Her feast day closely coincides with the original pagan celebration that marked the first signs of spring, Imbolc.

Believers in past Gods were dismissed as fools and heathens, uncivilised people who were little better than beasts. The new hierarchy had to be respected. The Pope and his priests rose to the top, above the kings and nobles. The poor and the meek stayed at the bottom.

As Nietzsche says, the creation of this thought system was a masterstroke.

The new currency of thinking cleverly took power from the aristocratic class and gave it to a small minority, who could then exercise enormous control over the masses — this box of thinking with its avenging God, universal sinfulness, and threat of eternal damnation. It made people servile. It made their lives empty and colourless. It told people they were blessed, but unworthy.

The Church's control was not only exercised in the royal courts of Europe, but in vast stone buildings, abbeys, cathedrals, and churches where the people listened with anxiety to the priests, who stood with their backs to the congregation and talked in Latin, as if those present were hearing an incantation and some miracle was in preparation. These buildings were intended to reflect power and inspire fear. The great cross always loomed large, a constant reminder of sin, death, and the chance of redemption.

People were told they were in need of salvation, which only priests could provide. They were not to compare themselves with each other, because this would not generate sufficient discontent, but only with this ethereal Being, this God. Every believer had to be distracted and troubled. Everything people did, everything they aspired to, had to be viewed through this God's lens. Every big and small experience was overshadowed by the risk of angering this God, with the threat of eternal punishment always present. People were imperfect, they were told, their greatest sin was being born. They should live in shame.

Personal freedom was drastically curtailed through this way of thinking, through fear and self-loathing. The majority became oppressed by the weight of their real and imaginary sins, and by the belief that only supernatural powers could offer salvation. The demands of this thought system were always impossible to achieve; they were excessive by design, so people could never satisfy them, and never be free. Happiness had a festering malignity, a narrow deadening quietude that could only be briefly attained.

This over-enveloping system of thinking ensured the intellectual energy of people was redirected, away from the feasting and pleasure of pagan rituals, towards regret, and a guilt for sinfulness that could never be assuaged, that was dispiriting. The souls of people became

filled with resentment, their minds populated with dark corners, tortu-
ous paths and sealed doors. Actions were led by prudence, not desire.

The old morality of kings and nobles had enhanced their ambition and pushed them to ecstatic bursts of rage, love, reverence, and
gratitude. The Church's ideas redirected this energy. They made everyone cautious, afraid for their fate. The old ruling aristocracy had not
taken itself, nor its enemies, disasters and misdeeds, very seriously for
any length of time. The new way of thinking bred small-mindedness,
a sense of meanness, enmity, bitterness and a desire for revenge that
could be passed down generations, a bubbling cauldron of unsatisfied
anger fed to every grandchild.

I am reminded here of the centuries of problems in Ireland, in
Britain's eternal distrust of Europe, and England's relationship with
Russia. Centuries of loathing carried down the generations. For what?

I find it impressive in some ways that human minds created this
thought box, this dangerous bait, with its corrupting influence on
thinking. The old lords and masters were pushed aside, while the morality and fears of the vulgar and uneducated triumphed, controlled
through a crude and greedy institution. It created a poison that ran
through the veins of European society, through the whole of humankind, for centuries. Much of it remains.

The worldview of the Church enslaved people. It encouraged them
to reject all those who were outside. Anyone who was different, an un-
believer, a believer in a different God, was an enemy. While the morality
of the older aristocratic class developed and expanded spontaneously,
at least among the ruling class, the new approach constricted thinking
for everyone. It shortened perspectives and redirected ambition.

This system of thinking remained dominant for centuries and, as
I've said, it still has tentacles embedded inside the modern Western
mind today. Eventually though, the thinking of science rose to challenge the ideas of the Church. Science became the next dominant currency of thought, the next thought system. It is the second currency I
will examine.

2 — The Thinking Currency of Science

I have written about this already, when I looked at the ethereal aspects of thinking. I will try not to repeat myself too much. You have my notes.

Like Christianity, science is a complete system of thinking, a *whole* view of the world, with all the elements tied together, a reality-philosophy that manifestly believes in itself alone. It has the courage to be itself, without the need for any support.

Science is a closed-minded system of thinking, unable to conceive of the notion that another way of thought might exist, or be superior. It has little useful to say about much that matters, and yet denies the possibility of any other approach. It mocks other worldviews as unworthy. It fails to consider the interconnectedness of all things. Science is a hiding place for disbelief, a mindset without morality. It excludes all it does not like, that cannot be examined in the language it defines, with a shake of the head, closed ears and eyes tightly shut.

You've said that my views are uncommon here, and that my concerns about science are overstated. What was it Nietzsche said about scientists? I think he summed it up perfectly. *"With all their noisy agitator-babble"*, these *"trumpeters of reality are bad musicians"*.[1]

Still, perhaps you have a point. I do not deny that science has brought humanity a great deal that is positive, or that it has a vital role to play. My concern is that science has taken too large a place in human thinking, far more than it should. I find the closed-mindedness of so many scientists hard to take, their unquestioning belief in their own methods, their own designs, their shutting out of everything that really matters. It doesn't take much thought to see that there is much that science can't explain, that it turns away from, or ignores. Its failure to understand consciousness, or thinking, for example. The universe is vast and complex, and there is so much that is not understood, that

---

1 Nietzsche, F., *The Genealogy of Morals*, third essay, "What is the meaning of ascetic ideals?", chapter 23, page 3.

cannot be understood this way. Why do we all have to believe science can explain everything?

Science replaced the thinking system of the Church, at least in part. Rather than one God, and a belief in the supernatural, its thinking is framed around proofs and the petty examination of the smallest things. In its efforts to explain everything in a different way, much that is important is lost. Science moves humanity forward in one direction only, because the scientific approach doesn't have any understanding of the nature of everything, not even a credible theory.

The approach favoured by scientists seems almost designed to prevent them from seeing anything but their own version of reality. It's a self-administered anaesthetic for the mind, just like the worldview of the Christian Church.

It's all so inconsistent. All this hiding of results, faking, doctoring, abridging, omitting, suppressing, inventing, falsifying and re-interpreting of reality repudiates any common sense. Science wants to inveigle its way into everything, even into places where it detracts from good thinking. Its theories and hypotheses are too often adopted as facts before they are tested, then changed when the evidence proves them wrong.

Many years ago I read a book[2] by an American journalist, Bill Bryson, on the history of everything. Have you read it? He's not a scientist; he's a journalist, and a very good writer. He explains great swathes of scientific discovery extremely well.

While it's a fascinating book, it's also an infuriating one. Every section follows the same formula, whether its about the size of the universe, the history of geology, the causes of earthquakes or why mass extinctions happen. It first introduces the topic and then reviews past thinking before explaining current thinking. In every case, it encourages readers to laugh at past thinking, to be amused by how stupid previous generations were, and to be thankful to modern science for

---

2   Bryson W, (2004) *A Short History of Nearly Everything*, Black Swan, London.

finally finding the right answers. At no point does he wonder if the current answers are the correct ones. It is amusingly tautological. He shows how past science got it completely wrong and yet believes current science has somehow got it completely right. He shows us that science constantly updates its worldview, and then ignores that fact.

It's this scientific worldview that has brought us here, to this place where humanity thinks it can control nature. Thanks to science, humans have been persuaded to think that they can have all the answers, or at least that they will soon have all the answers. It makes people believe that humanity knows what it is doing and where it is going, that invented technologies can fix every problem. It's as dangerous a way of thinking as I can imagine because it is leading humanity blindly astray.

As I said, look back to my previous notes on this as you wish, on the way science likes to fake it.

The third currency of thinking I want to explore is economics. It is really your area of expertise and you will see that my notes have borrowed heavily from some of your books, as well as our conversations.

3 — The Thinking Currency of Economics

When it refers to the monetary system, modern economics likes to talk of hard currencies and soft currencies. Adapting this thinking, we might say that economics is a hard currency of thought, harder than Christianity. It is stronger, harder to penetrate and oppose. Because it is the dominant system of thought in the West today, it is very hard for most people to perceive and understand. It is hard to see. It's like being aware that you are dreaming. It's hard to do. When it comes to economics, it's difficult to stand far enough back, mentally, to see the entire way of thinking objectively, as if from a distance. It's like asking a cell to work out for itself that it's part of a living being.

Like the Christian religion, economics is based on a set of beliefs. Followers have to *believe* what they are told, not question it. As with the Church, many of the claims made by economists are elaborate mental constructions that are impossible to prove. As with the Church, followers of modern economic thinking are followers of a faith.

While modern economics, or neoliberalism, is often attributed to Adam Smith, this is not really justifiable. There has been a great deal of reinterpretation of what he intended, and a great deal of invention and development in thinking since his time. Smith was not an economist. He was a moral philosopher and historian. There's a big difference. Smith's objective was to improve living standards and reduce poverty. Increasing output would help achieve this, he said. Modern economics has taken this basic idea and extrapolated it, warping it in the process.

Like science and Christianity, modern economics is an interconnected system of thought, a *whole* worldview, another reality-philosophy that manifestly believes in itself. Like Christianity, it demands a belief in one God. The economic God is the free market, which is an ethereal, invisible, mysterious power too. Unlike a religious God, it is possible to regulate the economic God, to manage it quite easily. Thanks to its otherworldly status, however, people are told this not possible, or certainly very unwise. Market intervention is regarded as heresy. Yet, it *is* actually a choice, despite what Western economists say. Business activities could be regulated in some way, or they can be left to the market, unhindered by intervention. It's a choice modern economics says should not be made.

For true believers of economic thought, the free market is the wonder of the age. It propelled America and the West to global dominance, and allowed hundreds of millions of people in China and elsewhere to prosper. It won the 20th century.

None of this is true, of course. But just as it is hard, and often dangerous, to persuade true believers that wine does not turn into blood, or bread into flesh, wars have been fought over such beliefs, with millions slaughtered. Were not all those violent regime changes sponsored by the World Bank and the United States in South-East Asia, Africa and Latin America in the 1960s not just Crusades by another name?

∿

Let's first review the key pillars, the foundations of this constructed temple of thought.

1.) The first, and most important pillar of economic thinking is that growth is the goal. This idea has become so embedded that it almost seems to have become the *de facto* objective of modern societies, of human existence. Any slowing in the rate of growth generates front-page headlines.

Part of this idea is that growth creates work, employment. Accepting this idea, however, is to misunderstand how economists calculate the rate of growth. Growth is *not* an increase in consumption. It's not a result of people buying more stuff. Growth comes from a rise in productivity. It comes from increasing output for the same, or a lower, level of inputs, from making more cars with the same number, or fewer, of people and machines. Economic growth is about improving efficiency, and one of the best ways to achieve this is through mechanisation. It is achieved through replacing people with machines or artificial intelligence. Growth does not always mean more jobs. It often results in lower employment. The thought that it creates jobs is a *belief*.

The focus on endless growth also runs directly counter to reality, to the boundaries of chemistry and physics. On a finite planet, there cannot be infinite growth in production and resource use. That's just logic. But economists have chosen to ignore this fact, and persuaded their flock to believe a cancer-cell philosophy. Endless growth is another *belief*.

Anthropologist Gregory Bateson points out that the focus on growth is also monotonic. When the same thing occurs in biology, in mechanics, and in social phenomena, it destroys the system. The species dies out, the machine breaks down, or the society deteriorates and disappears. Sustainable monotonic processes are absent in nature, from cells to complex organisms. Life casts them out.

I know this is an area of great frustration for you. People's minds have been carefully nurtured so they deny this. They've been manipulated. I have often had the same experience as you. Whenever I suggest to people that there is no need for economic growth, that it is possible to live in a steady state, in balance, in harmony, I am met by looks of disbelief. When I point out that the growth philosophy runs counter to history, common sense and simple logic, people start to dismiss everything I say, as if to question the validity of this tissue-paper pillar of economic thinking is unthinkable. They are not thinking, and they are certainly not thinking about *life*. Yes, the poor world needs a better standard of living. But that can be achieved in other ways. It doesn't require economic growth. It can be achieved through redistribution, for example. But economists have persuaded people that growth is the only way.

In striving for this endless economic growth, the planet is being scraped clean of resources at an accelerating rate. While some raw materials will last for centuries, others will not. At some point, as they are continuously exploited, humanity will hit a wall. The costs and the energy required to extract them will one day exceed the gains they bring.

2.) This mindset alone, this push to unthinkingly exploit the world's natural resources, as well as the pollution it causes, will make life hard for future generations. It runs completely counter to the ideas of Adam Smith and classical economics. In modern economics, the consequences of all the plastic waste that's generated, the air pollution, the melting icecaps, and the oil spills, for example, are completely ignored. Modern economists dismiss it all as unwanted side effects, and call them externalities. This is the second pillar of thought and it too runs completely counter to the ideas of classical economics. Again, followers have to *believe* that these unwanted consequences don't matter, when they do.

3.) As well as focussing on growth, businesses are expected to maximise short-term profits. This is the third pillar of economic thought. It is what the market demands, ever-higher quarterly returns. A failure to boost profits is punished with a decline in the value of firms, with the bosses replaced. The market's wrath descends.

Another consequence of modern economic thinking is widening inequality, though followers are expected to *believe* the opposite, that the system reduces inequality. By design, the rewards of the system accumulate in the pockets of the rich. It is how the system works. The profits go to those who have enough money to invest in businesses, or to lend to others. To try and explain this away, economists talk about the trickle-down effect, like tears on the statue of a saint, a miracle. They claim that wealth filters down into the pockets of the poor, thanks to the magic of the free market. The fact that this doesn't happen in reality, the fact that the rich get ever richer, is ignored. The trickle-down effect is another *belief*.

4.) A fourth pillar is the notion of free trade. Poor countries are told to *believe* in open markets, to sell their resources and labour without restrictions. In reality, this is mostly a cloak for exploitation, because this makes it impossible for poor countries to industrialise. Without trade barriers, they can't compete with the scale and technology of rich countries. All they are able to do is sell their raw materials and labour cheaply to the rich world. Free-trade thinking condemns the poor world to stay poor forever. Only China managed to escape this trap, by cleverly ignoring the fourth commandment. It protected its local industries from imports, and gave them time to develop. It also blocked the sale of many raw materials. For almost every other country, however, free trade has been colonialism by another name.

5.) The fifth pillar is that modern economic thinking demands little or no regulation. Again, this is a belief. People have to believe that this will produce the best long-term outcome for most people. In reality, a lack of regulation allows the finance sector to manipulate markets leading to financial bubbles, and businesses to exploit people and nature. It allows businesses to make false claims and produce harmful goods, such as foods or medicines with long term side effects. Some

countries have even signed secret trade deals[34] that make it possible
for businesses to sue governments for lost profits in closed-door courts
if they introduce legislation that constrains their activities.

6.) The sixth pillar is the idea of creative destruction. It is another
belief. Creative destruction is when businesses rationalise, relocate or
close, leaving thousands of people stranded without work. While the
economic priests say this destruction is healthy, and that it promotes
growth, it is rarely very creative, nor beneficial to those affected. Cities
that industries once underpinned and built are left to decay when the
tide turns, when the factories are moved elsewhere to boost profits,
their citizens abandoned.

Economists are clever like this, as clever as the Church. They use
clever words and smart expressions, like the "free market", "externalities", "the trickle-down effect" and "creative destruction", to cloak
reality, to disguise injustice, to allow the high priests to increase their
wealth without most people being aware of what they are up to.

Economists have also reinterpreted Herbert Spencer's idea about
the survival of the fittest to suggest it means only the strong survive.
This re-imagining is useful: it encourages competition and dismisses
cooperation, while suggesting that economics is somehow underpinned by the laws of nature. It is a zoological approach to human
development, based on the idea that the strong should destroy the
weak (who are no longer blessed). In the economic thought system, it
is the rich who are good, saintly,[5] sacred, and admired, while the poor
are feckless, lazy welfare scroungers.

As you know, this is not what Spencer meant by the term "the survival of the fittest" at all. He meant that those creatures which "fit" their

3   https://www.theguardian.com/business/2015/jun/10/obscure-legal-system-lets-
     corportations-sue-states-ttip-icsid.

4   https://www.theguardian.com/global-development/2025/mar/07/private-
     investors-ability-to-sue-governments-is-a-form-of-legal-terrorism-ending-
     this-system-is-imperative-aoe.

5   See Ayn Rand, the concept of Objectivism.

environment best, those best suited to their circumstances, are those that survive. He was talking about living in balance with the environment, not striving to eradicate others in a fight to the top.

More broadly, this idea that everything in life is a battle helps justify much of the West's aggressive behaviour. It favours war, conflict, takeovers, attacks, mergers and acquisitions, whether or not this is of long-term benefit to most people. It encourages the strong to use their feral power, validating their behaviour, like a conflict between carnivores and herbivores, a form of entertainment, a spectacle to satisfy animal instincts. It equates aggression with progress, with feeding the "blond beast", as Nietzsche puts it. All this divides and blocks human thinking. It makes any hope of sensible development, any hope of understanding, harder.

There are other pillars in this economic system of thought. We have discussed them often enough.

Do I overstate my case? Perhaps a little. I happily acknowledge the free market has merits, as does the thought system of science. Both have helped humanity achieve great things. The free market allocates resources more efficiently, most of the time. It strives to make everything in the business world leaner, to drive prices lower. This can often boost living standards in the short term. An expanding economy encourages investment and innovation. The system is also flexible, with the ability to respond to changes in supply and demand.

But economic thinking has hard limits, and these are often ignored. It tends to be wasteful, forcing companies to make goods that fall apart, so more can be sold. It also works less well in the long term. It works less well with basic infrastructure, in providing roads, railways and energy, for example. It rarely works well when it takes control of universal services, such as schooling, healthcare and defence. It fails completely when it's faced with problems like climate change, microplastics in the environment, or disasters like Fukushima, where there is a 60-year clean up, life-threatening risks, and little hope of any profit.

The system dumps the costs of these externalities, and so many others, on society.

Economic thinking brushes nature aside, allowing forests to be chopped down, seas to be emptied of fish, and species to be entirely wiped out, because the free market allocates them no meaningful economic value. It frequently destroys lives, in the name of efficiency.

In the 19th century, factory workers came together to fight exploitation and oppression. Doing that is harder today, and it seems to me this is deliberate. People are being brazenly exploited by this system throughout the world, and yet because everyone has been persuaded to think they must act as lone individuals, their focus is atomised. The endless talk of growth is dogma.

The social divisions this thought system creates are powerful, and often hard to see. It is a racist system, especially in Europe and the US. There is an inbuilt bias in favour of the Coca-Cola culture of white people, especially white men, the old warrior class, and in favour of Western culture, which is viewed as intrinsically better than other cultures. The rules and values of the rich world are portrayed as universal laws: democracy, the free market, capitalism, individualism, science, human rights, the sacredness of private property ownership, and unlimited technological progress. Christianity is in there too, as is a claim to equality of opportunity, which is never intended to manifest itself in reality. There is an inbuilt nostalgia for war and conflict, coupled with a belief that the present is always better than the past. The role and dignity of those who lived before, of people's ancestors, is dismissed as unimportant.

People are separated according to wealth, and the levels of progress the system defines. Being rich and materially obsessed is regarded as good. Those who follow another God, who want state intervention, and refuse the blessings of the free market, are viewed as enemies: the Russians, the Chinese, the Cubans, the Venezuelans, the North Koreans and others.

Modern economics becomes fate.

The focus on the individual undermines the chance for any collective identity too — ethnic, cultural, religious, and national, for example — which, paradoxically, impedes awareness of individuality. It leaves people without any anchor to define themselves. People are left to work out what their identity means for themselves, and often struggle. The push for individual liberty, which is labelled as freedom, can be a prison.

The system expects people to work out themselves what their nominal freedom is actually *for*. They are told there is freedom *from:* from state intervention, from constraints on their behaviour, from common responsibility, from ethnic or cultural attachments, from restrictions on what they say. They *believe* this freedom is real. The reality is that the state still wields enormous influence over their lives, as do large corporations. People are not free to act, nor to say what they want. They *are* free from many interventions that would be to their benefit; they are free from any meaningful wealth redistribution, they are liberated from the chance of collective action, and they are released from real equality of opportunity.

Nor are they truly free within their minds, which is what freedom was originally supposed to mean. Their minds are imprisoned by this economic worldview. Everything is contractual and technical, with the economy as destiny.

Nothing in the system explains what this constructed freedom is *for*. For most, it doesn't appear to be for anything much. They have the freedom to buy the latest mobile phone, to travel to places overrun with other tourists, to eat food that gives them diabetes and heart disease, to watch videos, to destroy nature. They have the freedom to be dutiful, undemanding consumers of whatever makes the best profit for the wealthy, regardless of the long-term social and environmental consequences.

The economic way of thinking, the economic way of living, has become "common sense", in Gramscian terms. It has become so normal and accepted that no one thinks about it. The values of the economic system of thinking are taken for granted, accepted as natural, as if they were universal.

Of course, these values, the push for endless growth, for individualism, the arrogant belief in "being the greatest force for good the world has ever seen", and all the rest are not eternal nor universal ideas at all. They are the thinking of just one culture, at one time.

For decades, the West has been doing everything it can to impose this thought system on everyone else. This is a source of considerable irritation to the peoples of Russia, China and the Muslim world. They believe the West is denying them their right to sovereignty, their right to live by their own systems of thought and development. This feeling has already brought conflict. It's what the war in Ukraine was partly about.

It appears hard for people in the West to understand that not everyone wants to adopt the Western way of thinking, the neoliberal economic thought system. Others see it as homogenised, lifeless. To other cultures, the West's behaviour suggests it believes they are inferior, that other peoples are imperfect. They feel that they are being told to modernise and standardise as the West dictates, and they don't want to. They think the West wants uni-polarism, uni-culturalism, universalism. They fear it means neo-colonialism.

Again, it seems to me that these other cultures may have a point.

In my second set of notes on thinking, I wrote about the notion of Being, about the essence of existence, and whether or not this could be equated with thinking. Seen through the eyes of other cultures, Western economic thinking looks more like a form of human entropy, the ultimate oblivion of Being. It comes across as that midnight where nothingness seeps through the walls. Because people are not thinking, they cannot Be. They are endlessly washed along by tides of emptiness, grasping for something to hold on to, a web of alienation expressed through technology, with nothingness on the throne.

Heidegger seems to agree. Neoliberalism is the "source of the calculative thinking" that lies at the heart of "Western nihilism", he said.

Thankfully, escape from this thought system is not too difficult. It only requires an awakening, for people to see that their minds have been held captive. Everything else is fixable. I'll come back to this at the end.

~

As with science, the economy is only a part of human existence. Like science, it offers nothing to guide us in what matters, except for the empty notion that people should profit financially from every activity. Economics has grabbed a far more dominant role in our lives than it should, by taking over almost every element of thought. Everything is a competition; everything is a market; everything must yield a monetary gain.

The worst outcome of this system is climate change. Economics' puffed-up unidirectional thinking is the direct cause of climate change. As you have said so many times before, it is the endless push for increased output that has created the problem.

For the economy to grow, more goods and services need to be produced. To power the factories — to provide the lighting, heating, computing and cooling — requires energy. Even today, after so many years of investment in renewables, more than 80% of this energy comes from fossil fuels. Even in 2040, according to forecasts by BP,[6] more than 70% of the energy used in the world will still come from fossil fuels. Burning these fossil fuels creates air pollution, greenhouse gases. This traps some of the sun's heat in the upper atmosphere. This causes climate change. The push for ever-higher output and the demands of this economic mindset are the direct cause of global warming.

This makes economic thinking much worse than scientific thought or the religious based system. The consequences of science or religion can be tragic, but rarely for everyone. Modern economic thought is suicidal for all. Unless societies can break free, unless they can learn to

---

6   BP Energy Outlook 2018.

think differently, everyone's fate is sealed. We are knowingly heading for a catastrophe, and yet most people cannot see that it is their thinking that is the cause.

How did this happen? By accident? Was modern economic thinking an inevitable consequence of a seed planted by Adam Smith 250 years ago?

It was not.

The system of thinking that dominates the Western world is the work of smart architects, spin doctors and public relations experts. It is the result of a "thought collective", deliberately set up "to change the minds of people".[7]

The process of changing Western thinking began after the Second World War, when a group of neoliberal economists formed the Mont Pelerin Society (MPS). Its goal is to spread free-market ideas, and what the group claims are the central values of civilisation. The founders were some of the 20th century's best-known economists, including Friedrich Hayek, Karl Popper, Ludwig von Mises, and Milton Friedman. It still operates today.

The MPS wants everyone to believe government and the welfare state are dangerous.

With generous funding from big businesses and wealthy individuals, the group came to popular attention in the late 1970s and early 1980s, when Margaret Thatcher and Ronald Reagan took power. Of President Reagan's 76 economic advisors, 22 were members of the MPS. In the UK, Prime Minister Thatcher's chief economics advisor, as well as many other economists close to her, were members of the MPS too.

Most economists in the Mont Pelerin Society are closely aligned to what is known as "the Austrian School of Economics", so named because the founders' families had roots in the Austro-Hungarian

---

7   Mirowski, P., & Plehwe, D. (Eds.). (2009). *The Road from Mont Pèlerin*. Harvard University Press. http://www.jstor.org/stable/j.ctt13xojdh, Introduction.

Empire. Originally, the term was intended as an insult, because mainstream economists saw their ideas as obscure and provincial.

Propaganda specialist Edward Louis Bernays, whose family also came from Austria, and who is better known as "the father of spin", played an important role in the development of the MPS too. His part was to encourage a sense of individualism, and promote an unthinking belief in what is called democracy.[8] Both ideas, as they are currently understood in the West, are central to Austrian School thinking. Individualism is easy to sell and undermines social cohesion. It reduces the chance of collective action. Democracy hands power to those who can influence the outcome of elections most: not politicians, but the media, big corporations and the rich. The system is called democracy and there are regular elections, which gives the people the illusion of participation. But the real voice of the people is kept weak while the role of the rich is enhanced.

There are people of influence outside the West, such as Alexander Dugin, who believe Western democratic thinking is more like a self-generating virus than a real system of governance. When it's applied to traditional societies, it frequently destroys them, causing them to descend into chaos. This is what the West intends. The West's promotion of democracy is just a cynical ploy, with deep, dark motives. It is a weapon used to extend imperialism, to divide other cultures, weaken them and then assimilate or exploit them.

They may have a point here too.

Still, these people, mainly from the BRICS countries, don't claim to be anti-Western, which is interesting. They say they are "non-Western".[9]

Within Western nations themselves, democracy has become like the soma in Huxley's *Brave New World*, a drug that keeps people content and unthinking, a stimulant issued to distract them from reality and what matters. Let the people get into a froth about those who wield

8　https://taz.de/Oekonomin-ueber-Meinungsmanipulation/!5585707/.

9　https://www.scmp.com/news/china/diplomacy/article/3302460/brics-not-anti-western-must-unite-against-external-shocks-chinese-think-tank.

very little power, and argue about the perceived variances between political parties that are near identical in practice. Let them think that ticking a box on a piece of paper once every four or five years is all that is needed to have their voice heard.

∽

The MPS has established a large number of pro-free market publishers and think tanks, to spread its ideas. These often offer employment to former politicians, bankers and journalists, people of influence who are selected because they are expected to encourage the spread of neoliberal thought. The group is also responsible for changing the way economics is taught in universities and schools. Rather than learning about a variety of economic ideas, as in the past, many of today's students are only taught about one system, neoliberalism. This encourages them to believe the neoliberal system should be universal. Only unthinking nations, those whose people live in darkness, cannot see this is true, goes the thinking, and they need to be enlightened by the West. The way economics is taught today encourages people to see the free market as a common-sense approach, neoliberalism as the natural order.

The MPS has also cleverly sought to influence the views of respected people who are not economists, those bungalow thinkers I mentioned earlier: doctors, scientists and lawyers, for example, so that these people become secondary carriers of neoliberal thought. Through targeted articles, documentaries and news reports, they become unthinking advocates of neoliberal ideas. Because their real expertise lies elsewhere, and because they respect the scholarly qualifications of MPS economists, they don't challenge the underlying assumptions of the system.

Do you remember Chien-Yi, that brilliant professor in Taiwan? Didn't you meet her in Taipei a few years ago? She wrote a book about the MPS. It's excellent. I especially love this quote:

"Immeasurable amounts of time, energy and talent have already been wasted on engaging [in] sincere debate with neoliberals as if they were honest theorists, thinkers, scholars, think-tank experts, or statesmen when actually, the core feature of neoliberalism is deceit."[10]

Despite this being true, the MPS has been very successful. Even environmental activists now frame their proposals in neoliberal terms. They offer market-based solutions to environmental problems because they have completely swallowed the idea that businesses should lead any change in society, and that fixing the planet should yield a financial reward. They rarely make calls for government regulation any more, because they have accepted the idea that market freedom is sacrosanct. It's quite comical, were it not so tragic.

Thanks to the pervasiveness of modern economic thinking, some environmentalists have even suggested nature should be treated as a financial asset. They want to give the forests, clouds, and the summer rain a monetary value, just like a factory or a machine. They call this "natural capital".

Didn't you write an article on this topic, with a plan to monetise kisses?

This monetisation of nature is pure neoliberalism. It is based on the idea that all decisions should depend on the economic value that will be lost or gained. If a cattle farm offers a better financial return than the "ecosystem services" a rainforest provides, it should be chopped down and burnt, goes the thinking. Environmental neoliberalism views the world as a commodity. Worse, it thinks humanity is qualified to decide nature's fate.

∼

I plan to finish my lecture on this topic with a quote from Guy de Maupassant's short story "Suicides".

---

10 Lu, Chien-Yi, *Surviving Democracy: Mitigating Climate Change in a Neoliberalized World*, Routledge 2020, Introduction, p. 2.

"We are the eternal toys of foolish and charming illusions, which are always being renewed."

If people understood how much their illusions are deliberately renewed by others, by those who have an agenda to profit from them, and control them, to change the way they think for their own benefit, most would surely be concerned.

Doesn't everyone like to think their mind is their own?

∼

Before I put my notes in an envelope and send them to you, I have one additional observation.

Having studied the ways thought has been deliberately manipulated for some time, I conclude that while it is relatively hard to change the views of one person, it appears easier to modify the thinking of crowds. Bernays was a master craftsman at this, the original father of spin, though I am not sure his legacy is one to be proud of.

As you know, I read news articles from a wide range of different sources. I seek out the views of other cultures and read what is said in other languages, to see how much unity of thinking there is, and how little. It's clear, I think, that there is manipulation of thought at the macro level, that people's minds have been deliberately shaped so they can be docile disciples in the church of neoliberalism, for example. There seems to be a lot of micro-level channelling too.

A couple of examples to illustrate what I mean.

In the UK, for more than 30 years, from the 1980s onwards, the local media drip-fed a message critical of the EU. It was frequently mocking. *The Sun, The Times,* and *The Daily Telegraph* newspapers were especially active, and particularly unbalanced, in this. Their framing, their narrative, was quite subtle at the beginning, but became less subtle. Whenever there was a difficult political or economic challenge, the EU was somehow to blame. While other European countries were critical of the EU at times, they stopped short of the kind of criticisms published in the UK. Many accusations levelled against the EU were completely false, downright lies. Boris Johnson was one of those who invented the damning stories that were complete nonsense,[11] but which shaped British thinking.

Unlike the UK, most other EU governments made considerable efforts to explain the benefits of EU membership to their citizens.

At the start, the UK's activities appeared relatively harmless, amusing even. Over the decades, however, the consequences of this drip-drip narrative grew until the balance of popular opinion changed. It played a large part in Brexit, in Britain's decision to leave the EU. Even today, nine years later, much of the UK media remains anti-EU, partly, I suspect, to try and justify what happened. They claim the EU is on the verge of a crisis, and that other countries want to leave too.

That is not the message I get from reading the European press. Some countries are critical of the EU but none are considering leaving. They see Britain's decision as a mistake, which objectively, from an economic and cultural perspective, it surely was.

What I am trying to say is that one side was led to believe something and the other side believed something different, but only one side knew this. The British were fed one way of thinking. They were not properly informed about opinions elsewhere, in Germany, Italy or France, for example, and they were not given objective information by their own government to help them form a balanced view. The British had one-sided thinking. This was not the case in the rest of Europe. People outside the UK knew what the British press was saying. They had the full picture.

Something similar has happened over recent decades concerning Russia and China. In the West, a message has been drip-fed to people that says Russia and China are hostile nations, a danger.

What is almost never discussed is what Chinese and Russian people think.

---

11   https://www.theguardian.com/politics/2019/jul/14/boris-johnson-brussels-bashing-stories-shaped-politics.

Of course, they see the situation quite differently. They believe the West doesn't understand them, that the Western media misrepresents them. They think it is the West that is being unreasonable and aggressive. They believe the West wants to force a system of economic thinking on them they do not like, and do not want. They fear the West's push for conformity, for assimilation and homogenisation. They see it as an assault on their cultures. They fear, and rightly so in my opinion, the West's colonial mindset, its belief that it knows better.

I have read books and articles published in the Chinese and Russian media that explain both sides of this story. The Chinese and the Russians are able to read about the views of people in the West. They know too that at some point there will need to be compromise, or there will be conflict. There will need to be discussions to correct this imbalance before the situation gets out of control. They know too that they will have an advantage if they understand the thinking of both sides. Those in the West are again being herded by one-sided thought. It will make compromise hard to achieve.

The West still behaves as if China and Russia are bad children who need to be trained to behave. They seem to think the Russians and Chinese need to learn to think like the West, to have Western democracy, Western notions of freedom, and adopt Western free-market ideas.

The West is not thinking.

∾

Thank you again for the comments on the first two sets of notes I sent. They have proved extremely useful. I will send you the fourth set of notes on how language influences thought very soon.

In the meantime, enjoy your trip to Brussels.

Much love
Max

CHAPTER 7

ON GIVING UP THE FIGHT — ENOUGH

Fragment from the Notebook of a Relinquished Global Citizen

T HIS ESSAY IS inspired by, and partly borrows from "Enough: Fragment from the Notebook of a Dead Artist", by Ivan Turgenev, written in 1864.

Enough.

'Enough', I said to myself as I moved with lagging steps towards the gate, down the steep walkway towards the quiet little corner of the terminal I knew so well. 'Enough', I said again, as I drank in the yeasty fragrance of beer and stale washcloths from the bar, strong and pungent in the decay of another falling evening. 'Enough', I said once more, as I sat on the stained bench above the loading bay, gazing at the clouds darkening over the taxiing aircraft, while they reflected the final rays of daylight.

No more struggle, no more strain. Time to draw back, time to keep a firm hold of the head and ask the heart to be silent. No more to brood over the sourness of vague, seductive hope, no more to sigh quietly at each laughably superficial easy-fix solution, no more to hang onto half-way thinking, no more to silently witness those smug advocates, those self-proclaimed protectors of the planet, deluding themselves that the way ahead is simple, self-evident and profitable.

All has been felt, by some, all has been gone through, by all.

I am weary. What is it to me, amid the soft peace of this distant corner and the glow of the evening, that three metres below, hidden by the bags waiting to be loaded, a diesel generator suddenly thrusts vast black plumes upwards, groaning in unearthly shouts, as though no such engine had been on earth before, and this were the first to sing its foul tune of accumulated despair? All this has been, and continues to be, endlessly repeated, with the hope that it will last forever, as though decreed and ordained, to lead humanity forward.

But into what?

Such thoughts would never have come to me once, in that time when I too was aflame like the sunset and my heart sang an entirely different tune, like a songbird. There is no doubt now; all can see that everything has faded; all life has paled. The light that gives life colour, depth and meaning, the light that comes from all our hearts, is dying within me and many others. Not dead yet, it feebly smoulders on, giving no light, no warmth.

The falling darkness is hungry to crush under its dead weight the last feeble rays of this impotent light. It is the way of darkness.

For the last time I drag myself from the cacophony around the boarding area down the narrow steel chute towards the plane, desperately seeking a silence to lie within. I turn a brief gaze again to the past, without any hope or prospect of its return, but also without any sense of bitterness or regret. What is now was always to be. This future is clearer than the intense blue heaven of a summer morning, purer than the first snows on the mountain tops. Spirited memories fade in slow procession, from gleaming marble to ruinous dust.

I am walking near a Scottish loch in winter, and the earth and sky are one unvarying milky hue, yet there is no haar. Not even the great hills that surround me stand out in the general whiteness. Distance is impossible to judge; everything looks both close and indistinct.

I walk swiftly over the ice-covered moss and, except for my own heavy breathing, cannot hear a sound. I think about the thrill of early spring, when the rain comes softly, and the hard ground begins to ease. I remember the glad tremor of my heart, that feeling which unexpectedly springs up, comprehended only by the soul, but vividly remembered now. It drew me forwards then, like a strong flood of light within me, without explaining the reason it brought me such pleasure, for why should it? It was like a swiftly opening flower, a sweetly bubbling Scottish burn, a pleasant shock, like the love of some natural wonder sparkling unexpectedly in the spirit, bewilderingly radiant.

Then I think of you, and many images float before me. They are of us, everywhere, in cities, in restaurants, on aircraft, curled up in bed. At every turn of my life, I knew you.

I stumble across the foundations of an ancient kirk, long given to neglectful mouldering. It is without any roof, just collapsed columns, a place worn nearly flat from the decay built on centuries of hopeful, unrewarded prayers. Where rows of packed people once knelt, only thistles remain faithful to this grave and melancholy remnant of belief.

We are alone here, alone in the whole world. Other than us, nothing is living. Outside, where these friendly walls of promise once stood, looming emptiness reigns. Chaos wails and moans, sightless eyes are weeping.

Within, beside you, there is still peace and light.

We nestle closer and lean our heads together. I feel the pulse of your blood. Your thoughts are my thoughts. Your smile is on my face before it's on yours, just as you say the answer before I ask the question. We are like two wings of the same bird, essential for flight and freedom. Our hopes have evaporated without ceremony, but they deepened our love. We have no need for words or looks to pass between us. Breath is all we need, for now, and to be together, barely conscious we are one.

The voluptuous melancholy, the tender thoughts, the smiles and looks that pierce our souls are above words. We sit in silence, heads bowed against the weight of feeling. I cannot forget it.

I am not able to give myself up from those memories, to bid them farewell. They are like the wick of a candle, flickering before it dies. Most remain unaware of the harsh hand humanity has dealt itself, and yet you and I are still foolish enough to imagine faintly that the deception has been lifted, that the shame and all those lies have been revealed in all their gallus deceit. The truth that permeates everything today is not a valid truth, not the full truth. But whenever we try to reveal it, we are not allowed to speak. They lock our lips and tie our hands. Nothing diverts them from their net zero.

The only way for someone to avoid the mire of the rapacious stupidity that characterises this Age of Endarkenment is to calmly turn away from it all, to say "enough". Then, we can fold our impotent arms on our impotent breasts and stand, defiant and broken. It is the last honour we can attain, a sorry consolation.

"*Our yesterdays have lighted fools, the way to dusty death, this walking shadow of life, that signifies nothing.*"

Still, eternity beacons.

I have become too soaked in knowledge, have feasted too freely from the tree of the knowledge of life, and have digested it all too poorly. I have tasted so much bitterness that honey is no longer sweet, and yet the bliss of love, of perfect nearness, of devotion, still gives much solace. The passion that glows, that murmurs eternal bliss, may yet devour the worm that consumes each withered tongue. Love still blossoms gratefully, if against the odds.

On that day when the grass is parched, when the dust and sunlight are endless, when summer is the only season, when all is bleached and grey, and the forests have gone, perhaps our love will remain. We all know, do we not, somewhere deep inside, that there will be no great words of consolation from any intelligence that was artificial, or otherwise, when freedom and progress are shown to be the apparitions they always were.

Were Shakespeare to be born again, he would find nothing new. Still the same motley crew, rolled out with the same terrifying sameness. The same sense of certainty, the same love of cruelty, the same lust for blood and gold, the same vulgar pleasures, the same senseless suffering, the same snares in which the multitude become trapped so easily, the same workings of power — the same small mouse turning in the same wire wheel. The tyrants of today, sitting smugly in their island lairs, in Zurich and California, so keen to broadcast their hollow achievements, who sleep well at nights while their half-crushed victims seek some comfort, will enjoy the same destiny as those they have so endlessly exploited, haunted like us all by the beauty that has been ruined.

What of art? Will that not remain? A clever Banksy sprayed overnight on a ParknShop in Wanchai is more real, and more powerful, than the Napoleonic Code or the symphonies of Beethoven, and yet each is the art of their era.

But art offers no eulogy. It is not the relativity of art that matters in the end, but its transitoriness, its brevity. Its transition to dust and ashes is what counts.

In their moment, and with their audience, art and beauty sometimes seem to have more power than nature, and appear more eternal. Yet only dull-witted fools can claim art is the imitation of nature. In the end, nature is inexorable. She has no need to hurry. Unconsciously and inflexibly obedient to her own laws, she knows no art, she knows no freedom, and she knows not good. From all ages, she suffers nothing that considers itself immortal, nothing that is unchanging. Humanity is her child, but she is the universal mother, and she has no preferences. All that sits in her lap today, all that pollution, those evaporating ice caps, that cough-inducing air, all will have arisen at the cost of something else, something humanity can already imagine but still appears unable to understand. Our uncivilised creation must soon yield its place to something else.

Humanity was perhaps too envious of nature's power. It appears that way. But, as humanity will learn, it cannot summon anything approaching the same forces by triumphing its empty conquests. Nature has the capacity to devour everything, unthinkingly. How can humanity resist the unceasingly rising tides, the withering heat and the endless rain? Does it really believe it can park hope in the value and dignity of those fleeting images sprayed on walls, in those sonnets? Humanity sits on the edge of an abyss, and has shaped barely nothing from dust.

Vanishing forms will not be averse to beauty. Beauty exists where humanity is not, where human freedom is not. Nature spoiled will come again. But humanity will not be repeated, and the work of our hands, our proud art and proud technology, once destroyed, will be lost. We were creators for just one hour.

What is left to say to the ordinary people, the second-rate and third-rate toilers, whoever they may be, the politicians, scientists, and artists? How can they be made to shake off their indolence, their weary stupor?

How to draw them back from the edge, when an idea has been seeded into their minds that denies the nullity of their existence? What would make them consider ideals higher than short-term gain, to want more than the destructive Mammon they have built for themselves? By what bitcoins can they be lured when their thoughts and achievements are so valueless? What can entice them to stop kneeling at the feet and grovelling before their new and lately discovered matinee idols? Do they not prefer to live in that marketplace where buyers and sellers cheat each other, where all is paltry and worthless? Do they not prefer to gape in open-mouthed adoration before sorry tinsel-decked images of progress? Why should they not be permitted to build a world where each egoistic self, alive with its own silent shouting, hurries feverishly to an already plainly visible end?

Why should they be denied?

Enough.

CHAPTER 8

WHAT IS THIS THING CALLED THINKING?

Part 4: The Role of Language in Thinking

HERE IS THE FOURTH part of my uncle's research on what is called thinking. This time he looks at how language determines thought.

∽

軒尼詩道
灣仔
香港
June 24

Dear nephew,

Your aunt mentioned that you found my notes on the subject of love.

Attached is my fourth set of notes on what is called thinking, on the role of language. I'm going to take a break next week and enjoy some time reflecting.

I'll write again soon.

慢走, as they say here, *man zou*!

Much love,
Max

∾

Part 4: The Role of Language in Thinking

What of language? How much does language determine what is called thinking? How much of what we call thinking is limited, or made possible, by the language we speak? What do the theories of linguistic relativity and linguistic determinism tell us? Is language the fabric of thought, as Humboldt claims? Language determines our worldview, he said. "*The diversity of languages is not a diversity of signs and sounds but a diversity of views of the world.*"

The nature of language lies in the relatedness of ideas words contain. That's a complex thought, a difficult sentence to grasp. I'll try to explain what I mean more simply. Every word has a meaning. Every meaning is related to an idea. Put all the words together and it forms a language. It is a living thing, a language. Words are constantly added, while others are forgotten, left to moulder in dictionaries. Who uses croton, finnimbrun or pintle these days?

The verb "to be" is an idea. It is the idea of existence. The verb "to have" is the idea of possession. The verb "to want" is the idea of desire or need. We learn the meanings of words as we grow up. When a parent wants a child to behave in a certain way, it's necessary for the word that contains the idea to be explained. A child must listen before it has understanding. Learning comes from thinking and understanding. It's a small thinking step that helps us make sense of the world.

No word can exist alone, because a language of one word is not a language. I am reminded of the thinking pathway I mentioned at the beginning, about how thought is a journey across an ever-changing landscape, a billowing ocean. Our thoughts are a process of discovery, and to communicate them, they become movement within a language.

How much does the language we speak create its own shifting ground? How much does it make the sea of thought surge and swell? Can it act like a damper on our waves of thought? Do some languages offer a smoother thought crossing than others? Is a language with more waves, which takes us across deeper waters, more poetic and refined than one that walks with shallow calmness?

If a language is unable to describe what is called thinking, explain what it is, how can the concept of thought be fully understood? When a language is uniformly available to everyone, what uniformity in thinking does this create? Does it constrain thinking by enforcing a particular way of thought?

Does someone with a mediocre vocabulary think less, or think less well? Do thinkers we might refer to as "crude", those who lack an understanding of many words, suffer from poorer thought? Is their vocabulary lacking, or their imagination, their ability to think?

Is there such a thing as pure thought, a perfect way to think? How much does the purity of thought depend on the language used?

For many years, it was believed those who spoke "superior" languages had superior thinking. While this idea is very little discussed today, because the implications are no longer politically acceptable, this does not mean the notion is wrong, nor right. Some languages, pidgin and creole for example, are regarded as simple. Though there is no specific ranking, it is clear that other languages have much more complex structures and much greater lexical complexity. Do societies with more complex languages achieve more? It obviously depends how we track it. If we use the measures of today, the size of an economy, the level of technological advancement, a sense of cultural superiority, the answer would seem to be affirmative. Cultures with complex languages are more successful. If we think about the societies that created the finest music, poetry and art, it appears to be true too. If we think about the cultures that have started the greatest conflicts, that have done the greatest damage to nature, then it is surely true as well.

Measuring language complexity is extremely difficult of course, as is measuring complexity of thought. Linguistics lacks any coherent theory of complexity. Most of the research on the link between language and thought is within the discipline of psychology, which surely boxes in what can be thought and said. The interconnections between language and thought are a question on which a cornucopia of disciplines could provide helpful insights, not just psychology. Neither language nor thought find their main intellectual home in psychology, I would argue. It may be a natural home for cognition, no more.

It is surely possible to demonstrate that some linguistic structures are more complex than others but that does not necessarily mean the thinking is more complex, or more advanced.

The German language has four cases and three genders while English has no cases and no genders. It is sometimes necessary for German speakers to hold a single sentence in their heads, which can extend to more than a written page, and which cannot be fully understood until the last word. This could negate the whole sentence or provide an essential verb to give it meaning. German speakers have to hold a lot of ideas in their head at once. Does this mean they think more, or better?

The Cantonese dialect in Chinese has nine tones, and it is very hard for those without experience of tonal languages to learn. Manlai says it is a language that evolves more quickly than most, with new word combinations and structures appearing all the time. But this does not necessarily mean it is more complex than other languages, from a thinking perspective. It is hard to see how this might mean Cantonese speakers think differently from the four-tone language used by most Taiwanese people, for example, especially when both use the same written script.

Does it matter if a language exists in written form? Some languages are only spoken. And, yes, this appears to suggest a lower potential level of thinking. When communication is limited to the spoken word, then the transmission of complex ideas is constrained by the intellectual and lexical limitations of the person speaking, their ability to comprehend and relate an idea. It is harder to verify what's being said without a definitive, written source.

Is it possible to think without language? A baby can respond to a stimulus without being able to say what's happening. It experiences the world at some level. Primitive humans, even without language and living in isolation, must have been able to think. Our minds are thinking constantly; it is impossible to stop the flow. Thoughts do not appear to us as words. How they appear is hard to say. How one person sees a thought may not be the way others see a thought.

We can probably conclude that it is possible to think without language, though only in a relatively limited way.

We can also surely agree that people brought up to speak different languages think slightly differently, at least to some degree, in ways that are not simply cultural.

In Spanish there are two versions of the verb "to be". One indicates permanence, the other transience. Death uses the temporary verb. This suggests Spanish speakers think a little differently about death compared to most English speakers.

In German, there are concepts expressed in single words, pillars of Germanic thought, that need several sentences to translate into English. German has several words for Being, awareness, consciousness, and existence that are hard to translate directly. The German word for passion is linked to the word for suffering, a derivation partly lost to contemporary English-language interpretations. The novels section in German bookshops is labelled "beautiful sadness", an idea that is strange to English readers.

In Chinese, there is not really any word for "no". There is only the negation of a verb. People say, "don't want", "don't have", "don't need", "not correct", "not alright", "is not", for example. Perhaps this suggests that Chinese speakers don't think as negatively as English speakers, not in such black and white terms. The Chinese response leaves a little more room for interpretation and discussion. It is a slightly different way to think, more nuanced. It's a slightly different way to behave towards others.

If a group of people who speak a particular language think slightly differently about a concept as simple as yes and no, perhaps they think differently about more complex ideas as well.

Similarly, in German, there is a word (*doch*) that can mean both yes or no, depending on the context.

The tonal nature of the Chinese language means multiple interpretations, and a great deal of humour, hidden in the homophones is lost in direct translation to other languages. The Chinese see a range of meanings in many sentences, and this would suggest they also think slightly differently. I imagine it must be a bit like colour blindness. A Chinese sentence can be red and green, either or both. One is never completely sure which is intended.

The number four is unlucky in Chinese because it is the same as the word for death, using a different tone, while the number eight sounds like another word which means wealth. So apartments on the eighth floor are worth more, while those on the fourth floor are rented out to foreigners, who are unaware of the bad fate that comes with their new home. A popular politician in Taiwan is known as "Korean fish" because this is what his name with different tones becomes. "Do you like Korean fish?" is a subtle way to ask about someone's political leanings. Thanks to double meanings, a man will never wear a green hat, because it suggests his wife has a lover, while to say someone is "eating soft ice cream" means a man is being looked after by his wife financially, which is not thought good.

Many languages retain the polite form of communicating, a mental construct that maintains a distance with strangers. Again, it is a different way of thinking, and relating to people. It changes perceptions of trust, and closeness. In German, there is a construction that allows someone to be quoted in a way that makes it clear that the person reporting takes no responsibility for what was said.

Can we say thinking is determined by language? There seems to be a strong case to support this idea. Different languages place different concepts in entirely different places. The thinking pillars of languages vary in significant ways, ways that lie at the root of understanding.

While German and English speakers have expressions that say being near a goal might as well be a mile away, the Chinese have an expression meaning exactly the opposite, that "nearly there" is good enough. In Singapore there's a word, *kiasu*, which means the satisfaction of winning when others are forced to lose. Because of this idea, Singaporeans sometimes take the best food from a buffet and throw it away, so others lose out. In a lift, they sometimes press the close-door button to frustrate someone approaching. Drivers block the exit road so those in the middle lane are unable to leave a motorway. These are all deliberate attempts to force others to lose, a way of thinking.

Do you remember Miyaki? She has a wonderful story about how the Japanese think. When the French built a high-speed train that went faster than the Japanese Shinkansen, the Japanese decided to re-engineer their train. They made it travel precisely 1 kph slower than the French one. Why? Because this sent a signal. Japanese engineers could easily make their train go faster than the French one. But to do so would be seen as crass and showy, unnecessarily competitive. Japanese engineers didn't need to do that.

I also remember going to a Toyota car showroom in Tokyo with her one day. I commented on the small hand-written signs on car windscreens, telling buyers about the car. I thought they looked a bit amateurish. Why didn't they print them out, and make them look neat?, I asked. She said this would not be seen by customers as friendly and approachable. It was a different way of thinking.

After, we looked at a large Mercedes car in a dealer selling foreign vehicles and the signs on the windscreens were neatly printed out. Then she shrieked in horror when she saw one of the buttons on the dashboard of the German car, the one used to recirculate the air. It was written in characters. "That's just so wrong!", she squawked. German engineers had adapted it for the Japanese market, thinking this was better. They had used characters for Japanese people to read. But Japanese people who drive foreign cars don't want that, she told me. If they drive a foreign car it must look foreign; everything must be foreign. That's what makes it cool, and distinctive, she said. Having a button with characters on it was just naff.

In Russian, words that express a sense of longing with nothing to long for, of boredom, melancholy, or spiritual anguish and yearning are closely interconnected, in a way that defies easy translation. While the Russian language blends conscience and morality with a sense of shame, Japanese thinking takes a different perspective. Face matters more than shame. The idea of being caught doing something embarrassing is more important to the Japanese than any thoughts about the morality of the act itself.

I had an American teacher of English at school. He taught us the plays of Shakespeare and was very good at it, except for one thing. He could never properly explain the meaning of the word irony. It's certainly a word that's difficult to explain and define, but it's also an idea that's essential to understand these plays. He had terrible problems explaining its meaning. It was as if he just couldn't grasp it. My friends and I wondered if it was a cultural issue. Was the fact that he was American the reason he didn't understand irony? When I watch American comedy shows, I sense the same problem.

There's an Alanis Morrisette song called "Ironic" where she sings "it's a black fly in your Chardonnay, good advice you just didn't take, or rain on your wedding day". She offers these as examples of irony. But none are good examples of irony. Perhaps the song is the problem.

Some societies dismiss ideas prominent in other languages as superstition, as if they believe their way of thinking is superior. They largely ignore the notion that people speaking other languages might be thinking and talking in metaphor. They don't really believe in dragons or elves, but they *do* believe in some force they are unable to otherwise explain.

In his book *The Tyranny of History*,[1] Jenner offers many insights into the differences between Chinese and Western thinking. While Westerners tend to look forward, he says, the Chinese tend to look back. People in the West are always focussed on what comes next, about their own plans and ambitions, while the Chinese view of the world is better imagined as someone walking backwards. Rather than seeing the past behind them, they face it, while stepping backwards. Chinese speakers are more concerned about their responsibilities to those who came before them. Their thinking is strongly influenced by what their ancestors did and achieved. The past is not to be undermined, but built on. It is a different worldview.

Similarly, Mandarin Chinese speakers think about time in a different way to English speakers.[2] Time is perceived more vertically. How does this change thinking, when time is a central idea to most languages?

Legal systems offer another example. The West prefers clear rules. Some actions are illegal, with each bad deed met with a counterbalancing penalty. As Nietzsche says, the Western legal system is essentially about revenge. Someone commits a crime and the state takes revenge by imposing a punishment that it says "fits the crime".

Legal thinking is different elsewhere. Laws in China are less specific, and designed to promote three interrelated concepts: China's worldview, China's values, and Chinese ethics. Laws are more inclined to express a general intention than a specific rule. The state expects people to behave in a certain way. They should not to be disruptive or act against the interests of others, for example. The laws reflect this broad intention, rather than having having hard-and-fast rules for every misdeed.

---

1   W. J. F. Jenner (1992) *The Tyranny of History: The Roots of China's Crisis.* London: Allen Lane.

2   Boroditsky L. "Does language shape thought? Mandarin and English speakers' conceptions of time". Cogn Psychol. 2001 Aug;43(1):1–22. doi: 10.1006/cogp.2001.0748. PMID: 11487292.

Similarly, thinking on the notion of freedom varies. This word, which seems relatively simple to translate, means different things in different places. In some societies freedom is about the chance to think without restraint. In the English-speaking world, it is generally about acting without restraint. In Russia, freedom can simply mean not being in captivity, while in Asia the concept of freedom comes with obligations to the rest of society and the family, because collective harmony is seen as more important than individual freedom. When American politicians talk of promoting freedom, the message received is not the message sent.

There are three other examples of differences in linguistics I will mention in my lecture.

1.) The way people think changes their views on government.

Variations in thinking can lead one society to embrace a particular political philosophy. A society that thinks individual freedom is more important than collective harmony inevitably requires a different po-litical, legal and governmental structure. When different cultures have different ways of thinking about how they should organise, it leads to misunderstandings not simply over the meaning of words but also about social goals, and the role and purpose of government. Different thinking can lead to disharmony between cultures.

Flexibility in thinking plays an important role here. In the West, some thought pillars are rigid. I examined this idea in my research notes on the currency of thinking. Ideas about free trade, economic development and light-touch regulation are deeply embedded in the West. They are not seen as *a* worldview but *the* worldview. They are an embedded "common-sense" way of thinking which dismisses any other approach. Common-sense thinking is not always good. It is the last resort of those who are envious of thinking by nature. Its sound-ness lies in its immunity from any accusation that it failed to address a new need. It has a rigidity that creates a block in thinking, an inability to consider alternative systems objectively. It is a glittering deception, with the pretence of being true and valid. It holds humanity back.

We all have a duty to shout out common-sense thinking when we see it, especially when it exists to make judgements on thought. How else will people wake up, unless they see what they are doing? Since the collapse of the Soviet Union, the idea that there is only one form of social and political organisation that works, the one based on democracy, liberalism and capitalism, has become fixed in the minds of people in the West, a common sense. This rigidity makes it hard for them to understand the thinking of others, or even to understand that a different way of thinking exists.

When a state-run society partially embraces some aspects of Western capitalism, as China has done, the West is confounded. It appears stunned, outraged. When China applies Western economic thinking, free-market liberalism, to parts of the economic system where it offers an advantage, but retains state direction where this offers other advantages, the West decries it as wrong. For the Chinese it is win-win, and perfectly sensible. For the West it is seen as unfair because it offers advantages the West doesn't like, or is not willing to think about. Western thinking on economics and politics is fossilised.

2.) The way people think changes their views on personal relationships.

In China,[3] the idea of getting married for love alone is not embraced. It is called a "naked marriage" because it leaves the couple exposed to financial instability. Two people coming together should always think about their future financial welfare and economic suitability. Love alone is not enough. Similarly, children are expected to support their parents when they get older. Looking after parents in old age is seen as a filial duty. Parents make a sacrifice to bring up children, and in return they depend on their children when they are old. These ideas reflect different values and opinions, and different ways of thinking.

3.) The way people think changes their approach to business.

---

3   https://www.mandarinblueprint.com/blog/15-chinese-words-that-dont-exist-in-english/.

In the West, businesses are expected to grow and focus on boosting profitability. It is not the same in much of Asia where profit is not necessarily the main objective of a firm. The primary goal might be to employ people, to provide a service to a community, or to support a family, for example.

∾

One final thought on the language of thinking, on framing, and propaganda. People in the West have been led to think that propaganda only exists in times of war, and mostly in other places. The reality is that it exists everywhere and always. Some people always want to change the thinking of others, in their own interests. The words that people choose change the thoughts of those who hear them.

When a country is referred to as a democracy, this is a code in the West for saying it is good. When it is not a democracy, it is called a regime, a code for bad. The word socialist is meant in a disparaging sense, to frame thinking negatively, even though the word simply means that government is organised in the interests of everyone, for society, while capitalism means government is organised in the interests of the rich.

Research to find a cure for cancer is called a fight or a battle, suggesting the disease is more likely to be fatal than others. The word sustainable is applied to products that are not sustainable at all. The word is ill-defined in any case, which is why it's used. What does sustainable mean, exactly? Nothing humans do involving the use of finite resources, or that creates rising pollution, is sustainable. Attaching the word is mostly done to give a false impression. It is a framing. Similarly, a new government policy that encourages personal responsibility usually means that people who once received support have been abandoned. Saying 80% of patients survive a treatment, isn't as bad as saying every patient has a one in five chance of dying.

Varying the words used, the language, like this is a thinking game which most are unaware is being played. That's the idea. It's another reason why people need to think more.

I want to come back to the word democracy as a final example. Democracy literally means rule by the people. As I've already mentioned, the word and the concept are sometimes used as a weapon by the West, to condemn or ostracise countries viewed as non-democratic. Some countries believe it is a governance system that is imposed by the West to sow chaos in traditional societies deliberately, to gain economic advantage.

There is also a framing here, which is important. The West only permits one interpretation of the word. To be accepted as democratic, a country must have several political parties, none of which is extreme in its views, and the people must have the chance to elect a government made up of these parties once every four or five years. That government then creates laws and makes other decisions, to fight wars for example, on behalf of the population, even when the ruling party is elected by a minority of voters, as is often the case.

Other forms of democracy are not accepted as valid, especially if there is only one party. This denies or misunderstands how other systems work. The Chinese government is democratic too: it just uses a different system. It is a system that thinks and calls itself democratic where people are voted into power and govern. Candidates are elected at a grass-roots level, for their village or community. Some are elected to represent business, the military, and other sections of society. Once in government, those elected rise within the party, generally on merit. Rather than a leadership with little or no experience of running a country, China is led by people who have been doing the job for decades.

I find it mildly amusing that, from the outside, many Western democracies and the US actually look very much like one-party states too, and yet they condemn China for that. In the US, there is very little to separate the Democrats from the Republicans, ideologically. They both stand for the same basic system — rule by the rich — capitalism, and US exceptionalism.

In Russia, despite Western media claims, President Putin is enormously popular, even after many years as leader. President Kim in North Korea is also hugely popular. This is not because they are dictators, or the opinions of citizens are manipulated and everyone is brainwashed. Just as Russia has a different system, North Korean society chooses a paternalistic style of leadership. Russians and North Koreans think it's Western society that's been brainwashed. They think the US, Europe and Australia are led by unqualified people who are puppets of a system of thinking, not true leaders. They say big corporations are in charge. The West's system is corrupt and manipulated by a small majority in their own interests, they say. Their evidence is compelling.

~

So, what is this thing called thinking?

We can conclude that what is called thinking is poorly understood, medically, linguistically and philosophically. It is one of the most basic of human functions, as vital as breathing and digestion, something which lies at the core of human consciousness, and yet it is barely understood at all.

We must conclude too that thinking is not the same as awareness. Nor is thinking a good word to describe the daily noise in our heads, which is hard to stop. Thinking requires effort, to actively consider the world and attempt to understand it. The endless chatter in our minds is a barrier to thinking.

Thinking defines us. It is Being. It is consciousness, the spirit, our soul. Thinking is a thing, an element, an activity, a way of being, that lacks most of the characteristics scientists and philosophers use to try to define it, which is why they fail.

When I spoke to Suzanna recently, and we talked about thinking, language, the spirit and soul, she said something interesting and unusual:

"Ich komme auch immer mehr drauf, dass wir Schöpfer sind! Und DARIN Gott ähnlich. Das ist so unglaublich genial. Wir könnten Welten schöpfen, erschaffen!!! Wir müssen es sogar tun! Schöpfungskraft!"[4]
She refers to what I said earlier, about the whole universe being present within each of us, when I talked about a living, conscious universe, developing and evolving around us, which we can all tune into. Is there a universal consciousness present in all living things? I asked. Is this what gives life? Do each of us have the whole universe within us, just as a fragment of a hologram contains the entire picture within it?

As you know, Suzanna has an otherworldly sense, and she feels strongly that this is so. She may be right. But what she said during our call is additionally interesting. She believes that we are also the creators of the world, that we create the world around us. More than that, we must create it, we must create the world around us. It is a calling, a need.

She may be on to something here. I think about *Siddhartha*, that wonderful book by Hermann Hesse, on the path to enlightenment and contemplation, on the need to surrender oneself to the irrational, about embracing the twisting, odd forms of nature until we find a sense of harmony with our inner Being, which appears as shapes, as our own creations, created by our moods.

The boundary between thinking and other worlds is very thin at times, and sometimes it can vanish. In another of his books,[5] Hesse puts it this way:

> To a great extent we are creators, our souls have a part in the continuous creation of the world. It is the same invisible godhead, which is active in us and nature. If the outside world fell into ruins, one of us would be capable of building it up again, for mountain and stream, tree and leaf, root and blossom, all that is shaped by nature lies modelled within us, comes from

---

4   "I'm also realizing more and more that we are creators! And in that, we are like God. It's so unbelievably brilliant. We could create worlds, bring them into being!!! We even have to do it! [We have] creative power!"

5   Hesse, H., (1919) *Demian: The Story of a Boyhood*, Fischer Verlag.

> our soul, whose essence is eternity, but which is revealed to us for the most part as the love-force and in our creative power.

Perhaps he is right. Perhaps we all contain the accumulated souls and knowledge of the world, of the universe. Perhaps this wisdom is somewhere within us, all the experiences of every soul that has ever lived, all those who were good and bad, the essence of every race and nation, all those desires, all those starting points, and the ability to create it all. If the world really is our own idea, as Schopenhauer says, then all this must be true. Everything we perceive depends entirely on our consciousness for its existence. Everything is a journey of the mind, a reality of exploration and discovery.

Yet I find people are afraid, scared of this idea. They are afraid of themselves, because they have never had the courage to Be, to be themselves. They are afraid of the unknown. At the same time, the laws they create no longer mean anything, and their commandments have become outworn. They know how to kill, how to pray, how to consume, and how to scroll, how to flick left and right, how to amuse themselves for a fleeting moment, and how to distract themselves from their empty reality for a short moment. But no cheerfulness or serenity can ever come from any of this. These creatures, who move so uneasily together. Their ideals have ceased to exist and yet they stone everyone who proposes anything new.

The pathway to something better is not difficult to see. Should people seek out that godhead, should they want to explore their inner wisdom, and become one with nature and the universe again, they have all the tools they need. They only need to think. That's all.

They need to learn to think again.

My final thought after all this research is this: thinking is difficult. It cannot be analysed using simple questions because misinterpretations threaten on all sides. That is because all mortal doings belong within thinking's realm.

∽

Well, dear nephew, this has been a longer exercise than I intended. I hope it has given you nourishment. I am tired now and must put all these books and papers away.

I am away next week, on my annual retreat at the abbey in Steiermark. I'll write again when I get back because there seems to me still one area I have not properly covered: the impact of AI on thinking.

With much love,

Max

∾

CHAPTER 9

ON THE IMPACT OF AI ON THINKING

Moray Place, Edinburgh
June 26

Dear nephew,

I have already sent you four sets of notes on thinking, on this thing called thinking, as Heidegger puts it. At the end of the last note I mentioned a gap I'd identified. I was concerned I had not sufficiently addressed the topic of AI.

I've given the issue some attention and enclose my notes.

Please let me have any comments.

With love
Uncle Max

~

I worry about AI. It is clear that there is more that needs to be thought about than ever before, and yet we are not thinking. A more complex world needs more complex thinking, and yet I fear AI will bring simpler thoughts.

A few months ago I needed to hire a car to drive from Munich to Salzburg and when I turned up to collect it, I was told the only car was a small Fiat. It was a dreadful little thing, like taking a step back 30 years.

I needed to visit a friend on the way and did not use the *Autobahn*. As the car had no satellite navigation I had to use a map. Much to my surprise, I found it quite difficult. When I had my own car a few years ago, using a map was no problem at all. I was able to memorise the route at the start, checking the map only when I felt something wasn't right. This time, I found it quite a challenge. I had to stop half a dozen times to be sure I was on the right road.

I concluded that my ability to remember a new route had been lost. I was no longer used to reading maps, and had lost the familiarity of this thinking.

Many people tell me they have the same problem with a pen. They are so used to their keyboards and phones, they've forgotten how to write. I see the same thing in shops. The assistants use calculators for the simplest arithmetic.

The same phenomenon exists with books. With more people consuming articles that take only a few minutes to digest, their ability to focus on something longer is waning. Concentration is being lost, and people are becoming easier to manipulate as a result. They are losing the ability to make judgements, do analysis and think. Just look at the lack of logic in many apps and websites. I sometimes wonder if the people writing them think at all. Often the most basic information is missing, or the steps required to do something are so unnecessarily convoluted as to drive the user to despair. I think of restaurant websites. There is always an obligatory page with a background story, some marketing nonsense about why their chef likes to cook. There are lots of pictures of their food. But if you try and find information about the opening times, or how to get there, it's hidden on some obscure page, and frequently out of date. It's infuriating!

I fear AI will make this sort of problem worse. The last remnants of many people's ability to think is being eradicated by machines that are not intelligent at all, despite what their designers claim. We are unthinkingly embracing programmed calculators billed as Nietzsche's supermen.

Of course, there are many areas where AI will prove invaluable. When I go to my doctor I am always conscious how little he really knows. He was trained 20 years ago, reads a few research papers each week, and knows a lot about common ailments. I worry what happens when he encounters something unfamiliar. I can only assume he starts to guess. I would far rather consult a machine that has all my medical history, which knows the symptoms of all known medical problems. A machine is more likely to give a correct diagnosis.

I am sure there are many other areas where AI will be of great benefit. It may help find cures for diseases. It might make products, food, and water safer. It could help us discover new forms of energy, or understand the universe a little more than now.

It's not only the impact of AI on thinking that worries me, however. I also worry about the consequences of rare events, when machines are faced with a problem and are unable to respond because they have not been programmed properly.

As you know, I worked with one of Europe's car makers for several years. I remember working on the prototype for a self-driving car. We made huge advances very quickly, just as Tesla and Google have done in the last few years. It's actually quite easy to build a self-driving car that is 95% safe. It's after that, it gets difficult. Making a car drive even more safely, just 4% more — that is safe 99% of the time — is a thousand times harder. The last 1% is a million times harder still. Engineers need to work through every possible risk, even those that are highly unlikely. They have to think about a child running onto the road when the sun is dazzling the system's camera, there is a large truck too close behind, wet snow on the road and the automatic windscreen wipers come on, smudging the screen and making it impossible for the driver to see. There are tens of millions of possible risks, and planning for them all is nearly impossible. This is why it is so difficult to develop a self-driving car that is safe. We eventually gave up.

The same risk is there with AI. It is not the 99.99% of solutions that AI can offer that are the concern. It is the 0.01% that it will get wrong that worry me, and their compound effect.

Societies need to think carefully about what they plan to do with AI, and they are not, because they are not thinking. AI is already having a damaging effect on critical thinking.[1] It is causing cognitive offloading, where people rely on AI tools to reduce mental effort. This undermines the development of analytical skills, and makes people think fact-checking and source analysis are not necessary. It reduces accuracy.

AI reinforces and amplifies everything worrying I have found in my research on thinking, on this thing called thinking. It is a substitute for thinking, a replacement. It purges minds that are increasingly running on near-empty, like buckets being rinsed of their contents.

Another concern is the impact of AI on what is called truth. AI makes it easy to create a false reality, to build stories using manipulated images and fake evidence, to show someone has done something or to create a spurious event. It reinforces mental echo chambers, confirms and strengthens false thinking. It diminishes long-term memory, reduces recall ability, and damages cognitive health.[2]

People are already citing what a machine has told them, believing they thought it themselves.[3] Their grip on reality has been weakened. There is a loss of cognitive autonomy, to use the proper psychological term, a loss of the self.

1   Gerlich, Michael. 2025. "AI Tools in Society: Impacts on Cognitive Offloading and the Future of Critical Thinking" *Societies* 15, no. 1: 6. https://doi.org/10.3390/soc15010006.

2   Sparrow B, Liu J, Wegner DM. "Google effects on memory: cognitive consequences of having information at our fingertips". *Science*. 2011 Aug 5;333(6043):776–8. doi: 10.1126/science.1207745. Epub 2011 Jul 14. PMID: 21764755.

3   Ward AF. "People mistake the internet's knowledge for their own". Proc Natl Acad Sci U S A. 2021 Oct 26;118(43):e2105061118. doi: 10.1073/pnas.2105061118. PMID: 34686595; PMCID: PMC8612631.

AI makes individuals more vulnerable to disruptions in technology and less capable of independent thought and action.[4] It reduces people's ability to reflect. Those with a high dependence on AI tools already score lower in critical thinking tests. As higher educational attainment is associated with critical thinking, AI is not just reducing thought. It is stupefying people. Thinking has become entropic. Instead of fossilising, it is decaying.

I worry too about the opaqueness of AI systems. They make it hard to know if something is fake, and almost impossible to prove there has been manipulation. AI makes it possible to deliberately change people's views, their behaviour, their relationships and their self-confidence, and impossible for them to show it ever happened.

There are AI tools that offer investment advice. Who designs them, I wonder, and for what purpose? People are applying for jobs and never meet anyone from the company they want to join. A machine ranks their application and then, pretending to be a person, interviews them. There are AI tools that write stories, compose music, and create art. There are several AI tools that create boyfriends for young girls, such as Candy AI, Anima AI, or Replika, "*the AI companion who cares*". These apps want to generate perfect partners, who do whatever the user hopes. There's one called Dream AI which is designed to explore people's fantasies.

We need to ask some vital questions here. Who designs these apps, and what are they trying to achieve? What data are they collecting, and for what purpose? What happens to the minds of the sometimes vulnerable young people who use them? How does it impact their lives, their relationships, and their thinking? Are these programmes not like drugs, another example of the soma mentioned in *Brave New World*?

Critically, what happens when these young people grow up? Are we creating a future society of empty-headed people with dreams that

---

4 Carr, N. *The Shallows: What the Internet is Doing to Our Brains*; W.W. Norton & Company: New York, NY, USA, 2010.

are impossible to achieve? Imagine how easy it will be to control them. Imagine what this will do to the structure of society.

Another concern is over the use of the word intelligence. I have read countless articles about the risk of machines taking over. Some are optimistic, others are not, but they all describe a world where big decisions will be made by computers, where humanity is governed or managed by its own inventions.

There is a deep flaw in this thinking. Yes, AI can learn and become better. But it cannot ever become intelligent. We must all remember that. It cannot ever become conscious. How can humanity create a thing it cannot even define? AI machines are as intelligent as a pot.

We also need to remember that AI is not a tool, as it is often portrayed. To call it a tool is a framing game. When people imagine tools, they think of chisels and spades and other implements that help those who work with their hands. AI is not a tool in that sense at all. It does not help people work with their hands. It takes away the need for them to work with their brains. It is not a tool to help a farmer. It is a mop to wash out thought.

I am fully aware that I may be too old to assess AI usefully and objectively. AI is still in its infancy. I am aware too that it is possible to present a completely different perspective. The skills people need in the future will be different. It's possible to imagine a future where people do not need to learn to read and write, or do arithmetic. It's possible to imagine a future where machines will write contracts and design buildings, where they will take on much of the role of government and policing.

It is also certain that humanity will face challenges requiring more thought than before.

It is possible to imagine AI could make humanity better able to cope with these challenges. It might enhance our abilities and analytical skills, to help humankind advance peacefully.

I am struggling to reconcile these contrasting ideas, however, because a positive outcome depends on where the process begins.

As they say, if you want to get there, don't start from here.

~

I value your thoughts. If you show this to other people, please tell them I wrote it. It was not done by a machine.

With love
Uncle Max

CHAPTER 10

ON MEANING AND PURPOSE

Taman Serasi, Singapore
July 14

Dear nephew,

I am feeling weary. The news reports are so endlessly upsetting, with so many precious lives being lost in endless, pointless conflicts. It is the foolishness of humanity, its inability to stop repeating history, that is so troubling. The momentum of human destiny is so obviously awry, so wantonly self-destructive, so devoid of thinking. It's the cycle of nature, I suppose, though it is hard to watch.

Can humanity ever break this cycle?

These days, I find that as soon as I sit down, I am drawn to this question, like a spiritual calling. Ideas flow into me, and I find I have a hundred things I must say, like a firework bursting into a dark sky, whether or not anyone cares to watch. Every book I pick up seems to offer me more of what I need. It's quite uncanny. Even so, this has been a difficult exercise.

To break the cycle, humanity needs to answer a slightly different question. What is our meaning and purpose? What are we all here for, and why? The search for purpose and meaning are eternal questions, of course, and they have no clear answer. Camus says the search for meaning is itself absurd. The arbitrariness of life means we cannot ever find the answer. While I fear he may be right, I wanted to give it a try anyway. Why not see if it's possible to sketch a rough draft of the answer, a hazy vision from all that has been written before?

As you read what I have written, please remember I did not construct the pillars of this thinking. That was done by others. As Confucius put it so wisely, I am just a transmitter of ideas, not their creator. I am not the font of knowledge. I am a small conduit, a receiver and forwarder. The ideas in my notes are out there, for anyone to find. I have changed nothing of their substance, nothing in their architecture. My footprint is that of an insect on the meniscus of an ocean.

Unfortunately, I have come to the same hopeless place as you.

If you can see how to move forward, let me know. It has been a rather upsetting exercise.

With love
Max

~

What is the purpose of human life? Why are we all here? Where are we going? What is humanity meant to achieve, collectively? What does our existence mean? Is something intended, or do we need to make it up as we go along? Is there some task for humanity, or is there nothing to do at all?

It may be wishful thinking, but I find it hard to accept that human existence is for nothing. Given the complexity of the universe, and its beauty, it is hard for me to accept the idea that humanity only exists to wage wars, have children, destroy nature, and open new department stores. A Beethoven symphony gets us closer to understanding human purpose I feel but, even then, there is surely more that can be achieved. Is there not some greater purpose to our Being?

Many people say we are the smartest form of life on the planet. That may be so, but I doubt it. Even if they are right, people can surely do more than try to manipulate DNA and slaughter their neighbours. Even if the world is an illusion, and the product of our own imagination, as Schopenhauer says, even if it is the creation of our own minds, that is no reason for us to be idle, to stop thinking. We can work to ensure our existence has some purpose, we can try to make our collective lives mean something, even if it is nothing more than an understanding of what is good and useful, even if it simply means that we learn how to live in harmony with the world around us, and our fellow creatures.

To give my analysis some structure and direction I needed a working hypothesis. From all I have read and learnt, I chose this: humanity exists to learn. It exists to learn what it takes to move beyond what is now, from what appears to Be. It is here to learn to think more, to become better, and for perhaps no other purpose than that. The task is simply to become better, to evolve a little.

By any useful measure, humanity has not moved forward much during the last 200,000 years. People behave much as they did hundreds of generations ago, despite so many technological breakthroughs and so much touted progress.

Humanity has not mastered the task, it seems to me, because it has not properly understood what it is to achieve. For there to be progress requires understanding. Humanity needs to understand what advancement means and it has failed to do this because it has not been thinking.

I started my search for meaning and purpose with the writings of Chinese philosophers, with Confucianism and Taoism, and with Indian Buddhism.

Taoism provides a particularly good place to start because it has long deplored a phenomenon that has been a feature of human existence since the beginning of time: the fruitless rivalry that comes from the individual and collective pursuit of power. This is the sand in the motor of the human machine, the friction that arises among people, the grit.

The pursuit of power is the trap that has kept humanity in the evolutionary shadows, kept it running endlessly around the same wire wheel. It is this rivalry that brings neighbours and civilisations into conflict. It blocks the path to peace and harmony. The pursuit of power, and all the attendant miseries it brings, the jealousies and greed, is the most crumbling and destructive force in human nature. It is the poison of human breath.

If humanity is to escape its whirlpool of deceit, if it is to avoid the conflict this rivalry creates, if it is to move ahead, the path is obvious, say Taoists. People must shed their snakeskin of enmity and rivalry. They must change their nature. Only then can there be real progress.

Changing human nature is something easily said, of course, a brief sentence of apparent simplicity that sits at the foot of a mountainous cliff ascending to the sky. How can humanity change its nature? Is such a thing even possible? It is so hard for an individual to change. How can an entire society, a whole species, change? How can humanity reverse endless generations of failed development? How can it shift from staying constant? How can it evolve into a species of some useful consequence, where human contentment is driven from the simple satisfaction of existence, of Being?

To achieve change on this scale will require a great deal of thinking and, as I've already written, that will be difficult when we live in a world of diminishing thought.

What are the conditions needed for better thinking? How can humanity prepare a seedbed for good thought? Does good thinking grow within democracies or monarchies, patriarchies, or paternalistic ways of living? Must societies invent something new, some new form of collective living, not yet imagined, if they are to think more usefully?

Defining what is needed is extremely difficult because the conditions required for better thinking are something humanity does not yet know. They are something that must be discovered. It will not be enough to eradicate weak thinking, non-thinking. Humanity needs to sense and search for something more, a worldview that propagates useful thinking, and this search will be harder than anything humanity has achieved so far.

Taoists believe the greatest barrier to human advancement is desire. Life is a ceaseless battlefield because everyone is under the bondage of desire. The main hurdle is not sexual desire, though that surely plays some part, but material desire. It is that grasping for pointless objects, none of which we can take with us after death, that foolish and nihilistic cycle of greed which most people are unable to control because they do not recognise its existence, or choose not to think about it. Even when they see it, and think about it, most people choose to control their greed and jealousy very little. That is because it is impractical, I suppose, a well-worn and ugly facet of human nature which most are too lazy to change.

Only by learning to think better can humanity move beyond this materially obsessed world. We first need to understand what is required to come into Being before we can explore any genuinely new development possibilities. We need to explore the senses that lie dormant within us, and understand the interconnectedness of everything. To understand that every human is a part of collective life, one of the obvious barriers that needs to be overcome before good thinking can prosper is the notion that humanity is separate from nature.

What then is the way forward? How can humanity usefully respond to the yawning abyss of meaninglessness? How should people deal with their everyday pain and suffering?

The modern solution, the Western approach, is to overfeed the source of non-thinking, to make the problem worse, to make people's brains bloated and unhealthy on a diet of ideas that lack any useful sustenance. It is through the banality of consumption, through denial of the problem, through drugs, alcohol, and a million other petty, meaningless distractions. As Nietzsche puts it, the modern solution is, "a little poison now and then: that produces pleasant dreams. And a lot of poison at last, for a pleasant death".

Taoists suggest another way. The way ahead, the path to banish meaninglessness, is through self-cultivation. It comes through a return to nature, by going back to an earlier state, just as the Christian Bible refers to the time before Adam and Eve, when there was paradise on earth, when the ruin of humanity began, when the seeds of greed and selfishness were sown. To escape our difficult destiny, to learn the art of living in balance with nature, and discover some inner harmony, it is necessary to become one with the living universe again. The answer is through the search for a reality that transcends language, time, space, and thought.

Taoism says we need to return to a state of stillness and protect that. Every living thing goes through a process of vitality and activity before returning to a state of stillness, back to its original state, back to its roots. To understand this cycle, to see the unchanging nature of things, is to be intelligent. It is to think. This realisation leads to the feeling of community. It takes us closer to heaven, or what we might like to call heaven.

Taoists believe a return to nature allows us to escape the problems and chaos that have been created by human laws, by the way people choose to live today. The social structures people have developed are flawed and fallible because humans created them. They were not created by nature. Humans cannot improve on nature.

This thinking sits in contrast to the ideas of modern science. Scientists behave today as if they believe humanity should try to improve nature. This is what drives them to remake and redesign parts of it. It is an approach that runs directly counter to the thinking of Chinese philosophy and Taoist thinking. Modern humanity's wrong-headedness and its problems are the result of its failure to understand this. In trying to discover the science behind the smallest particle, scientists have failed to understand the interconnectedness and meaning of everything.

It is not just in science that human thinking is failing. Flawed thinking is all around us. It is within human laws, inside the structure of our societies, seeded inside our values. It is our false ways of thinking and living that bind us within a "nutshell", as Shakespeare's Hamlet put it. Our approach to life fools each of us into believing we are the "king[s] of infinite space". They make us believe that we can understand, and master, the world around us. Our thinking lies at the root of human misunderstanding, and our inability to move ahead.

Escaping the babble of greed, and the imperfections of human existence, comes though "quietism", say Taoists. People need to learn to rise above the dust of ordinary affairs. Then, the desire for material possessions will fade and, with it, the risk of conflict. In a world without action, there can be no conflict. There is benevolence instead. Peace and kindness become duty. According to Lao Tsu, the old master, people need to develop a quiet receptivity. They need to learn to feel the workings of the Universal Spirit by listening properly to nature.

Confucian thinking says the search for meaning and purpose starts within ourselves and the family. If we can learn to properly cultivate ourselves, we will find enlightenment, and strength. If we look after our families, then the country will be in a good condition. If the country works well, we can build a world order based on peace.

It is said that political leaders have a duty to the people, while individuals have a duty to society and to their own cultivation. Everyone has a duty to contribute to the whole. Each small blemish keeps the whole from perfection. Personal integrity is the object of all people. Those who seek individual glory and profit are condemned. Confucianism says profit defiles our better nature. This does not mean people should avoid fame or gain. It means that such rewards should come to those who deserve them, to those who are virtuous, and have cultivated their character through literature, loyalty and faith.

Balance is essential in everything, it says. As it takes less effort, we should learn to move *with* the universe, not fight against it. Light needs darkness, strength needs weakness, male needs female. Female values, those that are cooperative, flexible, solid, and sometimes quiescent according to Taoism, are essential to complement the male qualities of activity and energy. Balance also comes through understanding the continuous cycle of life and death: the rigidity of death balances the weakness of life.

There are many other helpful ways of thinking here. The more someone searches, the less they understand. The flexibility and suppleness exemplified by water are superior qualities to rigidity and strength. Complementarity is natural, not competition. The empty space that is created within a cup for liquid, the space between the spokes of a wheel, the space enclosed by the walls of a room and the unpainted space between trees in a picture are all essential. From this nothingness comes function, usefulness.

We also need to know when it is time to stop. This idea can be interpreted to mean that we should let the world take its own course, that inaction can lead to change too, that it is sometimes wiser to let events move into the space that has been created. Everything has its own time and place. Force begets force; victory in war comes from destruction and is not something to celebrate; being rich does not enrich the spirit. Wisdom comes with the realisation that we know very little.

These ideas are reflected in Chinese art. Unlike in Western art, most of the figures that appear in classical Chinese paintings are not ordinary people. They are poets, people of virtue, those we should want to aspire to become. Chinese artists don't strive to create a perfect likeness of someone, but simply to indicate their dignity and noble-mindedness. Paintings of insects, twigs, birds and flowers reflect the intrinsic spirit of life, present in all things at their birth. Unlike Western art, there are very few depictions of evil or meanness. Nor are there satirical, mocking images. There are no Hogarths. Chinese landscape art encourages quiet reflection of nature, a spiritual contact with beauty, and a distrust of human knowledge and desire. Reality can only be understood by throwing out thinking, consciousness and knowledge.

To understand this thinking, it is necessary to empty the heart and lay it bare to the wonders of nature. As with nature, everything is always changing in our lives. We should learn to embrace this idea, not fear it, if we are to be happy. Only by seeing the vastness of nature can the heart and mind expand under the vision of such mightiness, and understand the nothingness of individual ego.

"All creatures under heaven are the offspring of Being, and Being itself is the offspring of Not-Being." Tao Te Ching 道德經, Chapter 40

Such thinking was once more common in the West. Until the time of Democritus, it was generally accepted, and unquestioningly, that the cosmos and everything in it shared in an inherent life, sentience and intelligence. This does not mean that every rock thinks and is aware of its surroundings. It is the universe that was thought to be alive, a consciousness that pervades everything we perceive, and all that we don't.

There are parallels in Western thinking about how humanity should develop too. It is as if this wisdom came from one great tablet of knowledge. Heraclitus offers an example. If people can cultivate their ability to observe, he said, the world will "speak" the truth to them like an open book. He coined the Greek word *logos* for the universal divine intelligence with which humanity can connect. The word literally referred to anything spoken, though the Stoics picked it up to mean the intelligence which governs the cosmos. It is the word used at the beginning of John's gospel where John writes, "In the beginning was the Word." It is the Tao.[1]

It is thinking.

There are many other similarities between Asian thinking, Christianity and philosophy. In the Zhuangzi, a foundational text of Taoism, the *Inner Chapters* talk about the coming of a great sage who will bring peace, just as Christian and Islamic prophesies talk of the second coming of Christ. These notions can be interpreted allegorically,

---

1   The Chinese Bible translates *logos* as Tao, the way.

so the saviour is not a person but a way of thinking. The way ahead is a voyage of self-discovery and reflection. This is how Nietzsche writes about his superman, his *Übermensch*, sent to save the last man, a way to think differently about meaning and purpose.

Other philosophies reach similar conclusions, often through a slightly different route. An idea that dominates, however, is that humanity cannot progress until it ends wars. War is the ultimate example of the failings in human conduct and false endeavour.

While Confucianism accepts the inevitability of destruction and conflict, of wars and individual enmities, it seeks to reduce their effect by binding societies through mutual dependence. It seeks to eradicate the causes of humanity's self-destructiveness, to end war. Buddhism seeks harmony too, with its sweeping rejection of the world, and its teaching of bodily forgetfulness, of realising emptiness, of seeing the world as a dream or illusion. It is only the shadows on Plato's cave wall that are real.

If people can understand that life and death are unimportant, that there is no intrinsic difference between people, that the world around us is an illusion, then the constraints on the soul can fade, and humanity can approach its original unencumbered state again, free from the world's wickedness. Only by standing out of reach of the world can we achieve any nobility of mind. The soul is by nature good but loses its way too easily in the material world.

Buddhists begin their search for peace through spiritual self-cultivation too, to embrace the universe. Finding enlightenment requires stepping back from the world, to bring light into darkness.

∾

From all I have read and thought on this most complicated topic, these ideas appear to me a good place to begin. They provide a hazy map to start understanding human meaning and purpose. We can all agree, can we not, that the goal of humanity, the ultimate objective of each of us, is not conflict, destruction and war. That is surely the antithesis of progress, of human evolution. These strands of thought provide a different way forward, by encouraging altruism and pacifism while suppressing egoism.

And yet... I worry that none of this helps us at all. I worry that all these thinkers and philosophers have come to similar conclusions because they have all been eating the same stew. I worry that what they tell us cannot work as we need it to.

I am reminded of those climate change goals we discussed. I think about all those people calling for the fossil fuel industry to be shuttered, about those who show how destructive our current economic system has become, especially for those who come next.

Such a change in thinking is simply not practical, even for those who understand the consequences. The idea of living in harmony with each other, and with nature, of eradicating war, of suppressing ego, greed and selfishness is surely a grand objective, but it is not realistic. There is no way for a transition in thinking to begin, with eight billion people and so much rivalry in the world. To misquote Kierkegaard a little, how do these ideas help people find a reason to get out of bed each morning? How do they give people a sense of meaning and purpose in the real world, in a world of jealousy, poverty, inequality, bereavement, and broken hearts. Where is that truth for *me* in all this? people will ask. How does this help people discover the meaning of life, *for themselves*? How is it possible to move from the real world, the day-to-day struggles that everyone faces, to this peaceful place?

I just can't see it.

How can those who argue for a different path encourage a change that goes against the way people live, which negates the values they live by? To build the foundations for such change would take decades. How is that useful, when the consequences of climate change are just around the corner? How does that help when these consequences will generate more friction in the world than anything that has come before? Who wants to make this sort of change when there is so much uncertainty and the outcome is so difficult for most people to imagine?

There seems so little reason for us to take a different path, and yet there is every reason to. The vast majority of people don't understand what's needed to slow the pace of climate change or radically change human behaviour. Most don't even understand why change is needed. They may not be content in their "nutshells", but they are unlikely to be quickly drawn to thinking that is easily dismissed as airy-fairy. Would their enemies not see such change as an opportunity, the chance to gain the upper hand?

Now, quite unexpectedly, I find I have come to where you are, my dear nephew, to exactly the same unhappy place, the same impossibly high stone wall. I feel lost. To move ahead, and believe in another path, another way, is to commit metaphysical suicide, it seems to me. It is to put all faith into a set of ideas, as a religion.

Now I feel that I am approaching the end of my arbitrary life without having found a way that makes sense that is not just crumbs of comfort.

∼

This is how my uncle's notes end.

I spoke to him on the phone after. When he refers to the impossibly high stone wall that lies ahead, he's referring to a feeling I described in the essay "Enough". It is the sense that there is no workable way forward, that to protect the heart it is necessary for the mind to step back, to preserve the soul.

My personal sense of hopelessness developed over the course of a decade. When I started working at the Club of Rome and learnt about the predicament of humankind, the Problematic, I was initially fired up, with a strong sense of purpose.

The book *The Limits to Growth*, published in 1972, made it clear to me that humanity was heading towards a crisis because of a series of interconnected, self-inflicted problems. The rapid rise in the population over the past 50 years coupled with the consequent demand for food and raw materials created more pollution — water, land and air pollution — than the planet could absorb. At some point, this would lead to a crisis. Despite the book's conclusion being mocked in the US, I could see it was factually inevitable. An endlessly rising population could not consume endlessly on a finite planet. The only question was about *when* this crisis would arrive, not if.

The book suggested the crisis would most likely begin between 2030 and 2040. Its consequences would last for many decades. Put simply, the entire system of human development would collapse and it would not happen quickly.

During my time at the Club of Rome, I also came to realise that the process of collapse had already begun, that the weeds which had been planted were beginning to sprout. This was obvious from the rising number of wars, from disputes over land, resources and food, increasing rivalry among the peoples of the world, and by an increased level of migration driven by need, not desire. The consequences of the rapid increase in pollution had created a time bomb. Air pollution was causing long-term changes in the atmosphere, while the accumulation of forever chemicals and microplastics was poisoning people, the land and the oceans. None of this could be quickly undone.

The conclusions of the Paris climate conference in 2015 made it clear that humanity must avoid a temperature rise of more than 1.5°C compared to pre-industrial times, yet we passed that level just eight years later, in 2023. Without a radical change in human behaviour, the concentration of dangerous gases in the atmosphere will pass another critical threshold in the early 2030s. This will be more serious, kicking off a chain reaction lasting centuries. It will gradually make much of the planet uninhabitable.

There is no way humanity can avoid this now. Nothing effective is being done to slow the buildup of gases, and the time remaining is too short for a transition on the scale necessary. Unless the world economy shuts down, crossing this critical and dangerous threshold is inevitable.

It also became clear to me that neither the Club of Rome nor anyone else in the environmental community was doing much useful to help humanity avoid these problems. Those involved were committed but also disorganised and unfocussed, while those on the other side, those responsible for creating the pollution, for financing the businesses concerned, all those in the oil, transportation and cement industries, and those pushing for more economic growth, were rich, competent and determined not to be diverted from their personally lucrative path.

That is why I left. I felt there was nothing useful that could be done.

Since then I have spent time trying to understand why humanity has failed to do anything useful to avoid such an obvious crisis, why societies would knowingly drive themselves into an ecological dead end. Why would humanity consciously take a path which it knows to be suicidal? I have found some answers, though they are of little practical help at this late stage, when humanity is like a cartoon character that has already run over a cliff, legs moving furiously, still with some forward momentum, but about to drop downwards.

My uncle, in seeking another path, in trying to find a different way forward, came to this same hopeless place, from an entirely different direction.

I do not accept his final conclusions, however. I believe he has found part of the answer, enough to help us move forward.

Here is the letter I sent back to him.

Dear Uncle Max,

I do not think you need to feel lost, or in despair. I think you have found the answer. The way ahead is there, just as you describe. The solution exists; it is there, ready for each of us to uncover, for each of us to discover. It is within each of us, and all of us collectively. You have taken us to the edge of that understanding.

You are perfectly right. We must change the way we think, and we must stop not-thinking.

I believe strongly that you and I, and millions of others, are on the correct side of history here. Because we can see, and because we have taken some time to understand, we know we are on the side of right. Hard as it is, we must make the leap onto a better pathway. Though it is difficult, and may be impractical, it is obviously correct.

It is clear from all you write that we cannot make this transition in one simple step, nor can we make it overnight. We first need to realise that a different way of thinking is necessary, and we need to see that this takes time and effort. Thinking is not easy.

We need to understand that the way ahead is a process, that it is a coming into Being. Coming into Being is hard. Today, we are like compressed butterflies trapped inside a vast thread of our own sour spittle, woven inside a shell we built around ourselves, which risks becoming our coffin. We need to focus on rebirth and see we need a metamorphosis. You have shown there is a way out. We are still pupa now, small immature insects, in the stage of development before adulthood. We need to see this, we need to understand, that's all.

That is the hardest part of the transition that lies ahead, as you've made clear. Understanding where we are takes thought.

What have we to lose? The world is, as you say, upsetting and already over the cliff. It is also clear from all your research that many great thinkers, many great people, have come to roughly the same conclusion, to the same wise place. They all see that the way ahead requires us to shake off the chains of our current way of thinking. We need to accept that change is necessary, and understand that we need to stop fighting each other. We need to learn to live together peacefully, and in balance with nature. These clever people did not come to the same conclusions because they were feeding from the same intellectual pot, eating the same stew as you put it. They lived in different parts of the world, in different centuries, and yet they all came to this same place, the same understanding.

They came to the same place because it is a place that makes sense. It provides a rough sketch of what is possible, a hazy guide for us to follow, a foundation to build from. These ideas can help people understand what happiness is, and what it is not. It is not grasping and greed; it is not conflict and material possessions. Your ideas can help us see what life means, what we can achieve, if we can learn to Be. Do not be discouraged, dear uncle Max, you have taken us to the edge of an answer.

Wisdom always sounds like foolishness.

Write more, please, and write again soon. I sign off with a quote from one of your favourite books, Siddhartha. It seems to sum up where you have reached rather well.

"The things you don't see... are directly in front of your eyes."

With much love
Graeme

∽

This essay was partly inspired by Chiang Yee's book *The Chinese Eye*, first published by Methuen and Co. in 1935.

CHAPTER 11

HOW OTHERS LIVE

T HERE IS ANOTHER planet in our solar system, just like Earth. It's
called Threa, and it is Earth's twin. This planet is impossible for
humans to see or detect because it is hidden behind the sun. Threa has
an orbit that is almost identical to the Earth's, just a little longer. As the
planet is a few thousand kilometres further away from the sun, it is a
little cooler, and each day lasts nearly 25 hours.

Half a million years ago, Threa would have been easily visible to
stargazers on Earth. That was long before humans existed, of course.
In another million years the planet will be visible again. It is unlikely,
however, any humans will be around to see it then either. So a whole
planet exists, and our species will never see it, nor know that it is there.

That's a shame, because humans could learn a lot from Threa. If
humans had known about this other planet and had copied the way
people there live, their time on Earth would have been very much
happier.

Threa looks a lot like Earth physically. It has blue skies, vast oceans,
and great swathes of land covered in breathing forests. Most of the
species living on the planet are similar too, and the people who live
there look pretty much like us, just a lot happier and healthier. They
live longer. There are a lot fewer of them, however, with their number
limited to a maximum of 500 million. Still, that's a lot of people, and
they all live well.

Human-like creatures first appeared on Threa about the same time as they did on Earth. But their society has developed differently. The Threan people took a different fork on the road and made different decisions about how to develop. They have had no wars for thousands of years. They have no cars, no internet, no weapons. They live contentedly together, sharing and appreciating what they have. They live sustainably and in harmony.

How did they achieve this?

The Threans started out much like us humans: hunter-gatherers living in tribes. There was enmity and conflict, especially after they started to settle pieces of land and began farming. When their feuds grew in number and the consequences worsened, the Threans did something difficult. They stopped making spears and other weapons, and the tribes sat down together to think about a different approach.

They could see that there was plenty of everything the people needed on the planet, and so the source of their conflicts was entirely irrational. So they decided to find a way to live together harmoniously. They scrapped all weapons and made it a social no-no to encourage or depict any form of violence, including violence against other species. They eat no fish nor meat. They established a system of government where absolutely everyone has to spend at least three years of their lives working in it, each time for a minimum of six months. This means everyone knows what it is like to govern, everyone has to contribute their effort and time, and everyone feels they are part of the system. They understand how it works and that it always needs to serve the long-term interests of the majority. Those who feel their personal short-term wishes are not taken into account understand why, and this makes them feel a bit better. Everyone is taught that the long-term needs of the majority are what matter most, because that is more harmonious.

After a few generations of working with this system they discovered a problem, a problem that is known as the "tragedy of the commons" on Earth. This is where people take advantage of the system to further their own ends, to gain while others lose. It took time to solve this problem. First, the Threans had to establish a set of principles, guidelines for all people to live by. Then they had to educate people to help them all see that selfishness is divisive. They also eradicated all forms of money and made everything freely available, based on need. Why steal, when there is no need? There are no laws on Threa, just principles and guidelines. There are no prisons either, nor any religions, taxes, or competitive sports.

There are no nations. There are towns and cities, groups that communicate extensively. Those serving in local government become eligible, after they have passed an exam, to work at a regional level. Those at a regional level can pass more exams if they wish to work at a higher level. Those who serve in government always have fixed terms and clear mandates. They are trained for the positions they hold. There are no political parties because efforts are continuously made to remove all and any sources of individual and collective friction or division. As the saying on Threa goes: rivalry is enemy number one.

As well as strict limits on the number of people, there are strict limits on resource use too. Natural materials can only be used if they fulfil two criteria: their use must not mean future generations will be adversely affected — they must have the same chance to utilise the same resources; and their use must not create any pollution which cannot easily be dispersed or absorbed by nature. Nothing should upset the balance of nature, nor adversely impact the ability of others to live well, even those not yet born.

Those who want to have children must apply, and are allocated the right on a first come, first permitted basis, so to speak. They are given the right to a child only when a space becomes available through the death of an elderly Threan. Though pregnancies without a permit are extremely rare, thanks to the sense of collective spirit and good methods of contraception, accidents do sometimes happen. These are terminated, and the couple is invited to apply for a permit. No one seems to mind.

Individualism is not encouraged, from an early age. Individualism is enemy number two, say the Threans. The self does not count. It is the collective will that matters. Of course, people can still be themselves. They just need to make sure that whatever they do does not harm anyone or disrupt social harmony.

The costs of living are very low, or they would be if there was any currency, any form of exchange. Housing, education, food, clothing and all other needs, including health and elderly care, are provided. There are no police, no armies, no courts, no judges, and no industrial conglomerates. Everything is done locally wherever possible. When there is a need for greater scale, there are collectives who come together, all guided by principles that have been refined for thousands of years.

As for work, because there is sufficient output, people only need to work for a few days a week. With the rest of their time they are encouraged to write, compose music and read poetry, teach others, or arrange festive events, large and small. Their music and literature are accomplished. Such imagination. There is alcohol, and it is freely available too, though any form of drunkenness or incapacity is heavily frowned upon if it risks upsetting the harmony.

Life on Threa is not perfect, and it takes a lot of effort. It all works pretty well though, and most people live happily.

Compared to life on Earth, it is a much better place to Be.

INDEX

OTHER BOOKS PUBLISHED BY ARKTOS

OTHER BOOKS PUBLISHED BY ARKTOS

OTHER BOOKS PUBLISHED BY ARKTOS

OTHER BOOKS PUBLISHED BY ARKTOS

www.ingramcontent.com/pod-product-compliance
Lightning Source LLC
Chambersburg PA
CBHW021506090426
42739CB00007B/483